Bridges
OVER
Ladders

*Secure **growth** & fortify **profit**
w/millennial employees & customers*

Kent J. Wessinger, PhD

Library of Congress Cataloging-in-Publication Data
A catalog record for this book has been requested

ISBN-13: 978-0-9998030-7-3
ISBN: 0999803077

www.create2elevate.com
kent@create2elevate.com

Cover design: Truth in Advertising, Atlanta, GA.

Printed in the United States of America
10 9 8 7 6 5 4 3 2 1

Kent J. Wessinger, PhD

BRIDGES
over
LADDERS

Dr. Kent Wessinger is committed to elevate nations, organizations, and corporations who are forfeiting growth because they are hemorrhaging their millennial workforce and muting their innovative ideas of value. In 2015, he used the outcomes of his globally acclaimed research on the transition from escalating crisis to sustainable growth in developing nations to establish the create2elevate research lab. Dr. Wessinger develops data tools to secure growth and solve the most complex problems related to millennial employees and customers in the financial services, risk management, human resources, education, and manufacturing sectors. As a keynote speaker and consultant, he has helped Fortune 500 companies, family businesses, and civic organizations secure growth and fortify profit with millennial employees and customers.

Kent has a PhD. from Prescott College in Sustainability Education with a research emphasis in economic sustainability within structures suffering from workforce migration; a Masters of Arts in Practical Theology from Regent University; and a Bachelor's of Science in Business Management from Kennesaw State University.

Other Publications:
Paradise Restored: Millennials determine the fate of "Paradise." Azura Press, Guyana.

The relationship between creative practice and socioeconomic crisis in the Caribbean: A path to sustainable growth. Routledge: London.

Millennials: Bridges over Ladders

ACKNOWLEDGMENTS:

To my mother Mary

"Strength and dignity are your clothing...and you do not eat the bread of idleness. Your children rise up and call you blessed; ... "Many women have done excellently, but you surpass them all." Proverbs 31:25-30

Sheree D'Egidio—Your attention to meticulous detail is without equal and greatly appreciated! Your excitement for life is infectiously undeniable. Craig is truly a blessed man. Thank you!

Millennials: Bridges over Ladders

Contents:

INTRODUCTION

Glossary:

Millennial = Born: 1982-2000
U.S. Census Bureau, 2015

Millennial truism: No demographic has ever been globally judged, parsed, or rebuked liked millennials, which has shrouded the term with a negative tone. Irrespective to the legitimacy of personal observations, millennials are reconstituting organizational structures that have been long defined as absolute.

Generation X (Gen X) = Born: 1962-1981
U.S. Census Bureau, 2011

Gen X truism: The confused generation … Hippies or yuppies? Greeks or geeks?

Baby Boomer = Born: 1946-1964
U.S. Census Bureau, 2010

Boomer truism: The accumulation generation. A house is just a place to keep your stuff … while you go out and get more stuff."

—George Carlin

Generation Z (GenZ) = Born: 2001-Present
U.S. Census Bureau, 2016

To all those who have labeled millennials as entitled, lazy, and/or selfish; here's news you may not want to hear…. millennials are having children!

BXers = Baby Boomers and Generation X

For this project, BXer is a term used to refer to both baby boomers and generation X. The two terms have been combined into one term, BXer.

WHY MILLENNIALS?

1. Largest workforce population on the planet (United Nations, 2018)
2. Highest annual purchasing power ever recorded (Brookings, 2018)
3. Recipients of the greatest transfer of wealth in the history of humanity (Forbes, 2018)
4. Occupy 72-76% of all tech positions (London School of Economics, 2017)
5. Most educated demographic ever recorded (Pew Research, 2017)
6. Average cost to replace one millennial employee is $30K (c2e NON-millennial survey, 2019)
7. Drivers of "local" (c2e Millennial ONLY survey, 2019)
8. Purpose driven (c2e Millennial ONLY survey, 2019)

This list is further expanded in Chapter #1; however, this project identifies many more reasons why understanding millennial perspectives and processes are critical to growth and profitability.

Noting that the oldest millennial will not turn 40 years old until 2022, millennials will continue to mature and assimilate into leadership positions in all sectors for the next 20 years, which suggests that sustainable growth flows through millennials for the next 2 decades. The outcomes of this project illuminate a well-defined path that will secure growth, fortify profitability, and position millennials as your greatest source of innovation.[1]

THE PROJECT:

As an educator, researcher, and resident in the Caribbean for nearly two decades, I was determined to ease the socio-economic crisis and develop a path of sustainable growth for the region.[2] Aware that the majority of the world viewed the region as paradise, I was struck when I learned that the region had the highest migration rate in the world for five consecutive decades.[3] While the majority of the world defined the region as paradise, those that lived in "paradise" were leaving at a higher rate than any other region on the planet. Seeking to comprehensively understand this phenomenon, I

---

[1] The data outcomes from this project have been implemented by three Fortune 500 companies in the financial services sector, global civic organizations, and numerous HR organizations; each who define the research as market leverage and proprietary to their growth.
[2] Wessinger, K. (2016). *The relationship between creative practice and socioeconomic crisis in the Caribbean: A path to sustainable growth*. Routledge: London, U.K.
[3] Ibid.

developed a qualitative project to understand, "*Why* are people leaving 'Paradise.'"[4]

The four-year project revealed that *self-growth* was the dominant factor for the high migration rate. In other words, if nations fail to provide environments, tools, and instruction for self-growth, people will migrate to nations where they can fulfill their vocational, academic, and financial potential. However, I was further alarmed by a peripheral reality illuminated by the project. Outside of the tourism sector; corporations, organizations, and the respective cultures were suffering greatly from the workforce migration, leaving little hope of reducing the socio-economic crisis in the region.

After publishing the research and developing the create2elevate research lab in 2016, I began to observe tendencies within the millennial generation that mirrored the central components of the socio-economic hardship in the Caribbean. Millennials are migrating from job to job at a higher rate than any demographic ever recorded, pressing corporations and organizations into an unexpected crisis mode.[5] The outcomes in this project reveal that millennials migrate from job to job at an average of every 18 months; whereas Gen X is 9.2 years, and baby boomers 19.1 years.[6] This reality, among other observed behavioral patterns with millennials, has created a deluge of written material. However, after purchasing 31 books on the subject matter, I discovered that each of them were primarily based on assumptions rooted in personal observation, not on the outcomes of an unbiased

---

[4] Wessinger, K. "Why are people leaving "Paradise?" TEDx Talk, British Virgin Islands, 2017.
[5] c2e Millennial ONLY survey, 2019
[6] www.create2elevate.com

and respected research structure. It was a deeply disturbing revelation to discover that companies and organizations were developing trajectories of growth about millennial employees, members, and customers utilizing opinions from biased observations.

Acting on the scarcity of respected research on the matter, I developed a quantitative research tool to extract the firsthand voice of millennials in contrast to baby boomers and generation X. As of the date of publication, the project has over 28,000 participants and the outcomes have been implemented by Fortune 500 companies, civic organizations, and national governments.

> *Without data you're just another*
> *person with an opinion.*[7]
> ——W. Edwards Deming

The growth of your company, organization, or nation will be determined by the decisions that you're currently making regarding millennials and their assimilation into leadership positions, which begs the question, *What data are you using to construct a future with millennial employees, members, and customers?* Bookstores and the internet are saturated with opinions and assumptions that conference speakers frequently quote as "truth" regarding millennials. Are you certain that you're developing your trajectories of growth on "truth" about millennials? Applying assumptions and opinions that are based on a few personal experiences have the potential to be devasting to any organizational

---

[7] Deming, Edwards (1993). *The New Economics for Industry, Government, and Education.* Ma: MIT Press, p.132

structure seeking growth. Through the two lenses that follow, this project provides you with critical information required to secure sustainable growth with millennials.

1. FIRSTHAND VOICE: This sustainable growth project is the firsthand voice of millennials, baby boomers, and Gen Xers.[8] This project is NOT assumption, theory, or opinion. The outcomes give you the opportunity to hear directly from tens of thousands of millennials, baby boomers, and Gen Xers to provide you with essential tools for sound decisions regarding the growth of your company, organization, or nation.

2. THE VALUE OF CONTRAST: In order to develop and secure a path of sustainable growth with millennial employees, members, and customers, this project utilizes the power of contrast. Contrast can be an effective tool that clarifies reality.[9] The positions and outcomes in this project are constructed solely by contrasting the firsthand voice of baby boomers/GenX to millennials.

---

[8] According to Creswell (2014) and Brubaker & Thomas (2000), surveys are a method that satisfies the criteria of a Primary Source in data collection. A Primary Source is classified as firsthand voice.
[9] The contrast effect is attributed to John Locke.
Uzgalis, William, "John Locke", The Stanford Encyclopedia of Philosophy (Summer 2018 Ed), Edward N. Zalta (ed.), URL = https://plato.stanford.edu/archives/sum2018

Development of project

Seeking understanding beyond personal observations and experiences, the surveys were developed in October 2016 with a single aim; contrast the social, occupational, leadership, financial, and environmental perspectives of millennials to those in the preceding generations.[10]

Scale of project

At the time of publication, 28,000+ participants have taken either the "Millennial ONLY survey," or the "NON-millennial survey."[11] The global breakdown of the participants is stated below.

Algeria	25+
Australia	300+
Belize	400+
Brazil	400+
British Virgin Islands	100+
Canada	3100+
Chile	50+
Costa Rica	200+
Germany	300+
India	500+
Iran	50+
Israel	200+
Lebanon	50+
Luxembourg	25+
Mexico	200+
Panama	50+

---

[10] The "Millennial ONLY survey" and the "NON-millennial survey" are located in the Appendix.

[11] Ibid

Philippines	50+
Russia	100+
Scotland	100+
Spain	100+
Sweden	100+
Switzerland	100+
United Kingdom	2600+
United States	18200+
US Virgin Islands	200+

Note: The participant pool also represents participants from 31 nations (not on the above list) with less than 25 participants.

Procurement of participants

Seeking participants, the links to both surveys were posted on LinkedIn, Facebook, and Instagram for 3 months. When the 500-participant mark was achieved, I began to present the research at Chambers of Commerce, civic organizations, and small corporations. Prior to the presentations, the members, employees, and/or customers were sent links to the surveys and requested to complete them prior to the research presentation. As the research continued to grow, the opportunities and sizes of the gatherings increased. Maintaining the same pattern of participant procurement, from January 2017 to December 2018 I presented the research in large corporations, Boards of Education, and executive gatherings in the United States and Caribbean nations.

OBJECTIVE OF THIS PROJECT:
Secure growth and fortify profit with millennial
employees and customers.

Smart people learn from everything and everyone, average people from their experiences, stupid people already have all the answers.

—Socrates

To fully satisfy the objective, this project seeks to … eradicate "average," diminish "stupid," and elevate ALL by "learning" from the firsthand voice of three generations; baby boomers, Generation X, and millennials. The future of your company, organization, and nation are too important to make complex and expensive decisions based on polished opinions found on the internet.

MILLENNIALS:
The GREATEST generation in organizational history?

Although some may find the suggestion laughable, I want to encourage you to assess the firsthand data in this project with an open mind.

TRUE or FALSE?

Is the leadership structure within your company, organization, community, or nation threatened by the conflict and influence of millennials?

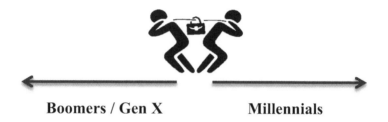

Boomers / Gen X   **Millennials**

Create a future with millennials, OR millennials will create a future for you!

Based on the outcomes in this research project, one outcome could fortify your legacy as a *champion* of leadership and growth, while the other could force *surrender* in conflict and crisis.

Why is the data in this project imperative to your growth?

Folly Point, Jamaica

Captivated by the beauty and tranquility of "paradise," Alfred Mitchell sought to impress his fiancé by building the most magnificent home in the Caribbean.[12] After purchasing the Folly Point peninsula outside of Port Antonio, Jamaica in 1904, his plan was to build a 60-room Roman villa that would be suitable for the pedigree of Miss Annie Tiffany. Yes, his fiancé was the daughter of Charles Tiffany, the founder of Tiffany & Co. in New York.

Having visions of carrying Annie over the threshold, he pushed workers to complete the house without delay, no matter the cost. Noting that he was insistent about completing the villa, stables, and saltwater swimming pool in the same phase of construction; the size and scale of the project required enormous amounts of fresh water to mix with the cement. However, to produce that quantity of fresh water in rural Jamaica in 1904 proved to be a complex dilemma that had the potential to significantly delay the project. To ease the barrier and secure a future in "paradise," Mr. Mitchell rationalized that the most efficient way to meet the timeline was to pump saltwater from the sea to mix with the cement.

---

[12] As with many stories in the Caribbean, intricate details are weaved with fact and folklore. Versions of this story can be found on many websites; however, this version comes from a personal tour of the property from a Jamaican historical guide.

Mr. Mitchell completed the house in his timeline, carried his wife over the threshold, swam in his saltwater pool, imported a Rolls Royce, and watched the sun set from the veranda each evening with his bride. However, after living in the house for 5 years, the house began to "mysteriously" crumble. The salt from the sea water was rusting the steel rebar inside the concrete and destabilized the structure. What once was an architectural marvel in paradise symbolizing strength and bliss, was quickly reduced to ruins and a permanent symbol of incompetency.

What is the correlation between a house built in rural Jamaica in 1904 and the growth of your organization with millennial employees, customers, and members? If you build your organizational structure on convenience, personal perspective, or longstanding cultural idioms; your structure might resemble a pillar of strength and bliss for a short season…your structure might even resemble "paradise" and draw millions of admiring people. Yet, structures built on faulty information will eventually deteriorate, crack, and collapse. When that happens, all fingers will point to those who made the decisions of growth based on unreliable information.

Want to secure a future of sustainable growth with millennials? Focus on the outcomes of data generated from the firsthand voice of a diverse and comprehensive population that speaks directly to the issue. This project has over 28,000 millennial and non-millennial voices that collectively speak to growth with millennial employees, members, and customers.

Thus, organizational leaders must answer one critical question; do you want your legacy of leadership to be one of sustainable growth, creativity and innovation, or a permanent reminder of incompetency? **Incompetency is a structure built on the justification of doing things "the way they have always been done;" while your innovative millennials migrate from job to job at record numbers.**

This project is specifically designed to equip leaders with the tools to make decisions that will fortify organizations with sustainable growth through the innovative ideas from millennial employees and members.

Chapter 1

lens2understand

the conflict w/ millennials

Question #1 in both the NON-millennial and the
millennial ONLY surveys:

*What is the first word that comes to mind when you think
of millennials?*

BEFORE *you turn the page and assess the results of the
surveys ... be prepared to focus on the contrast between
the answers from the baby boomer/Gen X and millennial
surveys.*

create2elevate.com
BABY BOOMER/GEN X
survey:

What one word best describes millennials?

(Top 6 answers from survey)
1. Entitled
2. Lazy
3. Selfish
4. Unreliable
5. Irresponsible
6. Spoiled

6k+ participants

create2elevate.com
MILLENNIAL
survey:

What one word best describes millennials?

(Top 6 answers from survey)
1. Innovative
2. Creative
3. Smart
4. Passionate
5. Progressive
6. Optimistic

22k+ participants

[13] These answers in both surveys have remained static for 2 years.

Critical Assessment:
Which one of the groups has the highest probability of securing organizational growth; the entitled, lazy, and selfish group, or the innovative, creative, and smart group? One seems to threaten stability, while the other could fortify certainty. One will seemingly squander resources, while the other seems confident they can add exponential value.

A lens2understand: Conflict of perspective

Shortly after graduating from the University of North Carolina at Wilmington, my millennial daughter Maggie wanted her voice to be heard. She loaded her car with camping gear and drove to Washington D.C. to march in the anti-gun protest following the tragic events in Parkland, Florida. The morning that she arrived she text messaged me a "selfie" standing in front of Trump Tower holding a sign that said, "I'm here so that my little brother does not get shot!" Exactly four minutes later, I received a text message from my mother (my daughter's grandmother), it was picture of her and my uncle at a gun range. My mother was wearing a Make America Great Again hat, with a caption that said, "I'm at the gun range shooting with your uncle."

There is no denying it, there is a confounding conflict of perspective between millennials and the generations before them. In spite of the cross generational differences in perspective, this project develops a model2grow, a strategy2profit, and a need2do-NOW with millennials. However, the path to growth and profit with millennial employees and customers begins with fully understanding the conflict. This chapter provides a lens2understand.

A lens2understand: To jump or not to jump?

When my close friend Jaco and I get together, our testosterone driven adventures fail to factor risk, which pushes his wife Catherine into her prayer closet. As residents of the British Virgin Islands, one Saturday we took our families to Peter Island for a day of rest and relationship.

Peter Island is a 20-minute boat ride across the Sir Francis Drake Channel, southwest of the main island of Tortola. The island is privately-owned and the home to one of the most exclusive resorts in the world. Although the island has suffered through hurricanes, droughts, and ship wrecks; the posh island remains a bastion for those seeking a quiet escape from reality (and a terrific dive shop)!

After completing our fatherly duties of snorkeling and lunch, Jaco and I decided that we needed to explore the island. A few minutes into our journey we were standing at the edge of a large cliff overlooking the endless sea on the backside of the island. Recognizing the massive rocks and ocean currents below us were too strong for snorkelers or recreational divers, we quickly surmised that the area must be pristine and full of natural wonders that few have seen. However, we were also cognizant that the experience came at a cost; if we jumped off the cliff into the water, we couldn't climb back up the steep slippery stone walls, meaning that we would have to swim to the other side of the island. We quickly made eye contact and understood with great clarity what our eyes were communicating…jump!

Falling toward the water, I distinctly recall thoughts that were rapidly flashing through my mind; what if I land on razor sharp coral heads and cut myself, will I become the source of a shark feeding frenzy? What if the currents are too strong and immediately push us back against the massive rocks, prohibiting us from swimming out away from trouble? My last thought prior to submersion was…What did we just do?

Once we were submersed, my flashes of thought became a reality, the relentless ocean currents pressing against the island were fierce. The large and magnificent coral heads were just a few feet from the surface, meaning that we had to time our escape with the waves. Each time a wave passed, the height of the swell would allow us to swim over another row of coral heads. If we failed to make it over before the wave withdrew, the swell would drop us on top of the razor-sharp coral head, leaving us cut and unable to move until the next wave arrived.

Twenty minutes after we jumped, we were able to make it around the eastern tip of the island and swim to safety in calm waters. Although we had small glimpses of the extraordinary beauty beneath us, our frantic pursuit to survive consumed all our energy and attention. Our focus was simple and exhausting; keep our heads above water and do not stop swimming, no matter how tired we become. As a result, **our experience was defined by the chaos of survival**.

When we made it fully around the Eastern tip of the island, we were stunned by what we witnessed. Right in front of us was one of the most beautiful and tranquil beaches we'd ever seen. The beach was protected by a coral reef and two long peninsulas. There were sunbathers down by the still water, hammocks tied to the layers of palm trees that separated the beach from the tropical canopy, and a West Indian chef preparing food on an open-air grill.

As we stepped out of the water, we both wondered how we could have missed seeing this remarkable area? The answer was revealed as we were making our way over the mountainous island back to our families. Just a few hundred yards up from the beautiful beach was the cliff from which we jumped. If we would have just denied the temptation to jump, walked a few more steps, we would not have jeopardized our existence.

Standing on that same cliff, once again we made eye contact and communicated a message of clarity...that was stupid! The reality of our actions revealed our foolish arrogance. Our decision to jump profited no one and threatened our existence.

As leaders contemplate millennial employees in their organizations, many leaders are standing at the edge of cliffs discouraged by the entitled, lazy, and selfish perspectives they hold for millennials. Jumping into the unknown and hoping for a good outcome might seem like a better alternative than turning over the "keys" of leadership to millennials. However, before you jump into the abyss of the sea with your "entitled" perspective of millennials, put down your perspective, walk away from the edge of the cliff, and demonstrate your astute leadership skills. Take steps forward by utilizing the firsthand voice in this project, then apply a process of critical assessment for growth and profit. Begin now!

Now is the time to compartmentalize your observations and look back at the attributes that millennials assign to themselves in the survey, then honestly determine if those qualities are essential to your growth. What type of person ensures growth for your company or organization? ... *entitled, lazy, selfish*; or *innovative, creative, smart*?

Growth does not come from entitled, lazy, and selfish people since growth is utterly dependent on innovative, creative, and intelligent people. Every company and organization have millennials who know they are innovative, creative, and smart, yet they are abandoning their post at record numbers because leaders cannot stop throwing the stones of *entitled, lazy, and selfish*.

If you can step away from the edge of the cliff, compartmentalize judgement, and keep walking for a short season, you will recognize that a future of extraordinary growth is right in front of you with a millennial workforce and customer base. This research project reveals how to retain millennial employees and members, master millennial talent acquisition, empower millennials to be thought leaders, equip millennials to be generators of innovative ideas of value, and become the driving force of growth. If you can't compartmentalize your judgement, take the plunge into the abyss, adapt to the chaos of survival, and discover that the sharks are hungry!

A lens2understand: Millennials reject what?

A widow once told me that rejection is worse than death. While the pain from death may fade, rejection is always in your face. Rejection is an open wound that is hard to heal and feels intimately personal.

34

Ground zero of the conflict between BXers and millennials is developed around rejection. Outcomes in the "Millennial ONLY Survey" definitively reveal that millennials reject longstanding methods and definitions of success established by the generations before them. However, the rejection is not personal, arrogant, or a character assassination; it's a conscious decision based on observations from a strategic seat. Let's be clear, putting a *lens2understand* on rejection, then utilizing the knowledge to wisely develop a path of growth, WILL define the future of your organization and the legacy of your leadership.

Therefore, securing sustainable growth with millennials is dependent upon an accurate *understanding* of the rejection. When millennial employees reject organizational structures that have been models of success for many generations, they are defined as "lazy or selfish." When well qualified millennials rebuff lucrative employment opportunities at successful companies, they are labeled as "entitled." Yet, understanding why millennials are widely rejecting established and sound structures requires an effort that digs deeper than personal perspectives and observations.

Based on the outcomes in the project and hundreds of face-to-face interviews with millennials over the last two years, I pose this question; "When millennials look back at their parents, grandparents, and the generations before them, what do they see?" Millennials see hard work, commitment, routine, sacrifice, and growth; all of which are attributes that millennials respect and appreciate. The most emphatically answered question in the *Millennial ONLY Survey* is, "Do you respect and adhere to the core values of the generations before you?"[14] The answer is shocking and unexpected to every non-millennial, 84% of the millennial respondents in the survey say they "do" respect and adhere to the core values from the generations before them. Further, the follow up question states, "Do you value the leadership wisdom from the generations before you?"[15] Again, every non-millennial is stunned when they see that 78% of millennials state they "do" value the leadership wisdom from the generations before them.

An assessment of the information strongly suggests that millennials are NOT rejecting the core values, nor the leadership wisdom established by the generations before them. Equipped with that knowledge, there is an underlying message here to all BXers. Millennials are looking to you for leadership; yet, throwing stones of "entitled, lazy, and selfish" is not the leadership model that millennials will follow.

Knowing that millennials move from job to job at an average of every 18 months, I'm aware that the core values and leadership revelation is a bit perplexing to BXers.[16] Thus, if millennials respect and adhere to the core values of the generations before them and respect their leadership wisdom, then what are millennials rejecting? The answer is *process*!

---

[14] At the time of publication, question #26 in the Millennial ONLY Survey.

[15] At the time of publication, question #27 in the Millennial ONLY Survey.

[16] c2e Millennial ONLY Survey

A lens2understand: Why do millennials reject BXer processes?

The generations prior to BXers suffered through oppression, depression, and World Wars. Each of those events destabilized financial security and negatively influenced everyday life. As those horrid events passed, people were resolutely determined never to be subjected to that type of hardship again.

Seeking individual and family security that would insulate them from decisions made by local and foreign governments, the generations prior to baby boomers forged a pattern of growth to insulate themselves from financial despair. The insulation was designed to protect them through retirement. That form of security was *accumulation*.

The *accumulation* of houses, parcels of land, savings, cash, retirement accounts, automobiles, and other assets represented layers of security. As more was accumulated, each new asset served as a new layer, an insulator of security. As the generations progressed, the embedded pattern of growth financially stabilized families, communities, and nations in layers of security. Today, when BXers assess the layers of their financial security, what do they see? They see a methodical process, a ladder of success that is climbed one rung at a time. Each rung symbolizes a greater sense of security that is insulated with more accumulation. As a result, the density of the accumulation determines the degree of security.

Make no mistake, millennials are fully aware that their generation has been built on the financial security that the generations before them secured. Millennials are cognizant to the reality that they are the recipients of the greatest transfer of wealth in the history of humanity.[17] However, nowhere in the surveys or my interactions with thousands of millennials have I ever heard a millennial question or demean that reality. Therefore, let me ask the question again, when millennials look back at the generations before them, what do they see?

Millennials see generations that meticulously climbed each rung on the ladder of success. Each step higher on the ladder demanded commitment, rigor, and sacrifice; which secured their lives through accumulation. However, there is another reality that millennials see when they look back at the generations before them—the glaring presence of dysfunction. This attribute is the source of conflict and the defining factor of why millennials reject the BXer method and definition of success.

No matter the level of success that BXers achieved, BXers will not be able to escape the mark of dysfunction. While BXers were working 12 hours per day to fill their buckets with material security; the family unit experienced breakdown like no other time in global history; divorce rates, crime, corruption, drugs, venereal diseases, migration and poverty all reached global highs with BXers. Tragically, millennials did not have to look back to see dysfunction, they had a front row seat.

When millennials assess the financial success of the generations before them, their first-hand observations solidify one reality; if financial security in that form comes with the dysfunction that I have witnessed, no thank you, I'll find another way to success!

When millennials place financial success and dysfunction on the scales of life, they see dysfunction as the dominant attribute spewing from the generations

---

[17] Brookings, 2018

before them. Equipped with a front row perspective of the dysfunction, millennials legitimately ask themselves, "If this is what the BXer ladder of success produces, why would I want to climb their ladder of success?"

So...what is it that millennials reject? Millennials do not reject the core values or the leadership wisdom from the generations before them, nor the end result of financial security; but they do reject the process that BXers used to achieve financial security. Millennials reject the ladder of success.

The prevailing response I receive at my research presentations related to this matter is, "The ladder of success is THE tried and true method of success. Who in their right mind would reject the only way to achieve growth and financial security?"

BXers that are baffled or offended by the rejection of the ladder of success, which is the majority, you have a critical and urgent decision to make. What is more important, the core values and end result, or the process utilized to achieve the end result? If your answer is, "The end result and the process cannot be separated...the process is what produced the end result;" aren't you really saying that the only way to achieve financial security is through the way that it has always been done? Ask yourself, "Are you willing to forfeit growth with millennials in order to cling to your process? Are you willing to waste the creative and innovative talents of your millennial employees, members, and customers by steadfastly holding on to your process of, 'My way or the highway?'" If so, your organization will remain isolated on an island named Conflict, while the island named Growth quickly expands with innovation and influence. The decision is yours![18]

---

[18] Case study: Growth Island vs. Conflict Island; Appendix A

Prior to us moving on to a model2grow with millennials, it is imperative that BXers understand that millennials want the same growth outcome as non-millennials; however, they are consciously choosing to take a different route to achieve the same results, which is fully discussed in subsequent chapters in this book. Noting that great leaders plan, sacrifice, and facilitate growth; if millennials astutely see a different route to the same destination, one that produces healthier outcomes, why would a great leader push back? Sustainable growth is sustainable growth. Fortifying profit is fortifying profit. Healthier is healthier.

VEXED BXers!

Due to the implications and intensity of the subject matter, I am inundated with frustrated BXers communicating the following statements, which always begins with three words;

"Those damn millennials …."

… have lost touch with reality!

… want to live in their parent's basement until their parents die!

… want it all handed to them!

… don't know what it means to work!

… aren't willing to start at the bottom and work their way up!

… want to travel the world while the parents pay the tab!

… are obsessed with self!

… want to be stroked and coddled to feel
accepted!

A lens2understand: Opportunity or Threat?

Make the decision based on the following 12 statistics

1. Recipients of the greatest transfer of wealth in the history of humanity (Forbes, 2018)
2. The highest annual purchasing power of any demographic ever recorded at $3.36 trillion, which is projected to reach $4.5 trillion by 2020 (Brookings, 2018; London School of Economics, 2016)
3. Millennials have 42% less credit card debt and 13% smaller mortgage balances at the same stage of maturity as baby boomers and gen X (U.S. Federal Reserve, 9/27/18)
4. 81% make purchases based on "word of mouth," yet nearly 77% define "word of mouth" as social media (c2e Millennial survey)
5. Highest educated demographic ever recorded; by the time the youngest millennial reaches 25 years old (2025), nearly 6 of 10 will have a bachelor's degree, compared to 35% of Gen X and 19% of Boomers (Brookings, 2/2018)
6. Millennial student loan debt is approaching two-trillion dollars (U.S. Treasury Dept, 10/18)
7. Largest workforce population on the planet (United Nations, 2018)
8. Occupy 72-76% of all tech positions (London School of Economics, 2017)
9. Millennials migrate from job to job at an average of every 18 months, which is a higher rate than

any demographic ever recorded (c2e Millennial ONLY survey)

10. Average cost to replace one millennial employee exceeds $35K, 11% of the respondents say it costs more than $50K to replace one millennial employee (c2e NON-millennial survey, 2019)

11. Define the age of adulthood as 28 years old (c2e Millennial ONLY survey)

12. Purpose driven (c2e Millennial ONLY survey, 2019)

The answer is …

Millennials are my greatest _____ !

Threat - OR - Opportunity?

A lens2understand: Millennial perspectives from +22k firsthand voices in the survey:

Boundaries
Millennials do not view the world as fragmented units, but as a whole unit. Millennials do not see nations, sexual orientations, or races; they see people.[19]

Environment
Millennials passionate concern for the environment is reflected in the organizations they seek out for employment. While 60% of millennials state that environmental responsibility is a filter used to select employment, 63% state they environmental responsibility is an ongoing assessment that factors into retention.

Food
Millennials are driving the organic food sector and local farmers markets. Assuming that pesticides, fertilizers, and preservatives are in our food; should millennials be judged for "overspending" on food to ensure long term physical and mental health?

Travel
Millennials are reconstituting the travel industry. BXers cannot fathom traveling halfway around the world to stay in the spare bedroom of a local family; I.e.: Airbnb.

---

[19] Although some verbiage may suggest blanket statements that are reflective of 100% of the respondents, no question in either survey has a 100% response rate. However, any statement perceived as a blanket statement in this project speaks to outcomes with a 75% or greater response rate.

Millennials are not seeking an experience based on the delusion of a creative facade; they're seeking a holistic experience to add depth to their lives and stability to local families in other cultures.

Millennials are…

- Rejecting the manufactured experiences of hotels for a holistic experience with a local family
- Supporting local families in other cultures
- Developing relationships with families in other cultures
- Learning and respecting local cultures
- Saving money on travel

Investing/saving

Millennials have the highest student loan debt of any demographic ever recorded; yet that is where the debt ends. Millennials are the most frugal demographic since the Great Depression generation. Their debt loads are low, while their investing/saving ratios far out exceed the BXers at the same stage. However, their justification for investing/saving is not motivated by retirement. Millennials set aside financial resources for holistic experiences throughout their lives. Millennials are NOT seeking to end life with an accumulated bag of money; they ARE seeking to end life with a lifetime of holistic experiences.

Innovation

No longer is innovation reserved for first world nations seeking profit and comfort; millennials have injected their holistic perspective into innovation. Millennials are intentionally reducing hardship for marginalized people in developing nations through innovative methods of communication, medicine, and education.

Education

Millennials are the highest educated demographic ever recorded. Recognizing that 58% have bachelor's degrees nearly doubles GenXers and triples boomers.[20] However, as BXers remain steadfast in their opinion that higher education is not for all, millennials are using their education to effectively elevate and advocate for all people. No longer is the objective to receive an education to advance to a higher rung on the ladder of success. The educational objective for millennials is to improve as many lives as possible with the knowledge gained from their academic achievements. Further, due to millennial attendance, trade school enrollment is booming.[21] Millennials seem determined to use their minds and/or hands to elevate the whole.

Self-growth

If there is no opportunity for self-growth, millennials move from job to job until they find that opportunity. The survey also reveals that self-growth is developed around the fulfillment of purpose. Millennials define fulfillment of purpose as having the opportunity to elevate the whole.

Holistic success

Millennials do not view a holistic lifestyle as a flippant fad of irresponsibility. From the millennial perspective, an intentional holistic lifestyle seeks sustainable growth for all components of life.

---

[20] Brookings, 2/2018
[21] NCES.ed.gov, 2018

- Is there fault in respecting the whole?
- Is there fault in seeking to elevate the whole?
- Is there fault in seeking a lifetime of holistic success?

Identity

There is NOT a success divide between BXers and millennials; there is an identity divide. Based on the analysis of the surveys, two distinct identities have emerged:

BXer Identity = Accumulation
Success is measured through accumulation

Millennial Identity = Holistic
Success is measured through holistic wellbeing

The BXer identity has produced undeniable growth and stability, but has also yielded pockets of debilitating conflict that threatens sustainable growth. The millennial identity is an intentional response that seeks growth by elevating the whole, which they define as healthy growth.

In case I have failed to clearly communicate...the largest demographic on the planet with the highest annual purchasing power ever recorded and benefactors of the greatest transfer of wealth in the history of humanity, is leaving Conflict Island and headed to Growth Island. Irrespective of size or scale, the migration of millennials is having a monumental impact on organizational structures throughout the world. Those that fail to wisely manage the migration conflict will not survive, but those who put down judgment and recognize that relevant creativity and innovation are essential components for sustainable growth will thrive. Do not be a fool and pridefully bury your company or organization on Conflict Island with an "entitlement" perspective of millennials...fortify your growth by building a bridge to Growth Island! However, ladders cannot reach Growth Island and token bridges to "nowhere" only produce expensive outcomes of failure. If you are seeking to fortify sustainable growth and secure long-term profitability for your company, build the bridge to Growth Island now!

If I have done my job, hopefully you *understand* "Why" millennials are leaving Conflict Island; the remainder of the project is dedicated to "How" to build a relevant **model2grow** with millennials, and "How" to develop a **strategy2profit** with millennial employees, members, and customers.

SNAPSHOT of Understanding:

Entrepreneurship

The millennial ONLY survey reveals a historically low 2% of millennials prefer entrepreneurship over the umbrella of an established organization. That is a stunning revelation since 17% of BXers select and prioritize entrepreneurship.

47

CHAPTER REVIEW: A lens2understand millennials

- There is a *confounding conflict* of perspective between millennials and the generations before them

- Many BXer leaders are standing at the edge of cliffs discouraged by the entitled, lazy, and selfish perspectives they hold for millennials

- Millennials do not reject the core values or the leadership wisdom from the generations before them, nor the end result of financial security; but they do *reject the process* that BXers used to achieve financial security

- Millennials want the same growth outcome as non-millennials; however, they are consciously *choosing to take a different route* to achieve the same results

- BXers must decide if millennials are a *threat or an opportunity for growth?*

- There is NOT a success divide between BXers and millennials; there is an *identity divide.*

Chapter 2

model2grow

w/millennial employees

What methods do you utilize to retain your millennial employees in your workforce?

A. Pay increase
B. Position promotion
C. Increased voice
D. Fringe benefits
E. Other

BEFORE *you turn the page and assess the results of the surveys ... be prepared to focus on the contrast between the answers from the baby boomer/Gen X and millennial surveys.*

create2elevate.com
BABY BOOMER/GEN X
survey:

What method do you utilize to retain your millennial employees?

1. Pay increase   39%
2. Position promotion   28%
3. Fringe benefits   25%
4. Other   7%
5. Increased voice   1%

+6k Participants

create2elevate.com
MILLENNIAL
survey:

What is the number one reason why you left your last job?

(Top 4 answers from survey)
1. Not heard   38%
2. Pay   33%
3. Freedom to create   16%
4. Benefits   13%

+22k Participants

Critical Assessment:
The surveys reveal that a whopping 92% of current
BXer leaders are utilizing one of three "tried and true"
methods in an attempt to retain their millennial
employees; 1) increase in pay, 2) position promotion,
and/or 3) additional fringe benefits, while millennials
prioritize *voice* as the most important factor for
remaining on the job.

A model2grow: Replace the confounding conflict

Being a single parent of three millennial children has been
confounding and marked with perplexing moments
related to our differences in perspective. Shortly after my
youngest son Sam started his senior year of high school,
he informed me that he had a girlfriend that lived in a
town about 30 miles away from our home. He wanted to
make certain that he had permission to drive back and
forth to see her.

Four months into their relationship, I received a
call from Sam at 1:30 a.m. As many can testify, panic is
the response when you receive a late-night call from your
teenage child. When I hastily answered the phone, I was
expecting the worst. Sam immediately said, "Dad, don't
panic, but I have a problem. My map app on my phone is
not working and I'm lost." Puzzled by his problem, I
answered, "How many times have you driven to
Rebecca's house?" Sam said, "That's not the point Dad,
my map app is not working, and I am lost." I said to him,
"Then what's the name of the road that you're travelling
on?" He repeated, "I do not know. My map app is not
working." Finally, I said to him, "Are you traveling North

or South?" He replied in a frustrated tone, "MY MAP APP IS NOT WORKING, DAD!"

Knowing that everyone reading this book has perplexing stories related millennials, let's not forget that millennials also have stories about BXers. **There is no denying it, there is a confounding conflict of perspective between millennials and the generations before them**. Employee loyalty and retention is the epicenter of the conflict. However, the outcomes of this research project unequivocally show that growth and profitability are dependent on millennial employee retention, yet millennial retention is dependent upon a respected *voice*. It's time to replace the confounding conflict with a voice of growth.

A model2grow: Converting voice to growth

We are on voice overload. It seems impossible to escape the barrage of voice that is inundating our lives. We have 24-hour news outlets that cannot stop screaming at one another, political parties that are constantly warring, personalities on social media fighting for our attention, and hashtag protest movements begging us to join their cause. Further, YouTube reported that in 2018 there were 500 million users that uploaded 400 hours of video every minute of the day.[22] Frustrated by voice overload, I am desperate for all those voices to "shut up" for a moment so that I can breathe. How about you? Therefore, adding another voice to all the noise seems irrational and antagonistic.

Based on the +22k millennials participants in the survey, the number one reason why millennials are

---

[22] www.brandwatch.com/blog/youtube-stats (Retrieved, 2/2019).

moving from job to job every 18 months is, "not heard." Be clear, millennials are not demanding a *voice*, millennials are leaving when there is no opportunity for *voice*. Before we jump on our entitled, lazy, and selfish bandwagon, lets qualify the *voice* that millennials are seeking. The voices coming from news outlets, political parties, social media, and protest movements all have one prevailing message; they are demanding change. Whereas, the *voice* that millennials are seeking is defined by growth. If I change a rolling chair for a stationary chair, the functionality may be a bit different, but it's still a chair. **Change is not growth and rarely makes any difference**. However, trees produce fruit when they grow. Females produce offspring when they grow. Organizations scale when they grow. Growth and change are perpendicular realities. BXers must choose, growth or change? Millennials are seeking growth and requesting a voice at the table to create, innovate, and elevate. If their request is denied, they take their talents elsewhere. It's time to convert the voice of your millennial employees into growth.

The proof is in the ~~pudding~~ voice!

A model2grow: Moving beyond tried &true

When Martha Millennial informs Jerry GenX that she has received an offer to join another firm, the firsthand voice in the surveys suggests that Jerry GenX immediately offers an increase in pay, a promotion, and/or additional fringe benefits. Once those 3 "tried and true" methods of retention have been agreed upon, Jerry GenX pats himself on the back and believes that he has retained Martha Millennial as a valuable employee for years to come.

As absurd as this question sounds, "Why did Jerry GenX use the 3 "tried and true" methods to retain Martha Millennial? The obvious answer is…they are "tried and true!" However, reality suggests that Jerry GenX used those methods because they were effective motivations for *him* to remain on his job for several decades. Ten years ago, when Jerry GenX had a competing offer, Ben Boomer retained Jerry GenX with the same methods. Jerry GenX assumed that the "tried and true" methods that retained him were irrefutable principles that transcend the generations. Jerry GenX was wrong!

Making the matter worse, millennials freely accept the generous "tried and true" offerings with a bright smile and a word of appreciation, then use them as a baseline for their next job. Although the longstanding "tried and true" methods of retention seem to be rooted in an unshakable trajectory of growth, millennials continue to migrate from job to job at a higher rate than any other demographic ever recorded. In comparison, the average baby boomer remained on the job 19.1 years, the average GenX remains on the job 9.2 years, yet the average millennial only remains on the job for 18 months.

It's time to move beyond the "tried and true" methods of retention. The outcomes clearly indicate that the "tried and true" methods were effective for a long period of time; but are now highly ineffective for the majority of millennials. Again, millennials are rejecting the BXer processes of growth and success, which seems to be a catalyst for one of the most repetitive statements I hear from attendees at my conferences, "Who the hell do those entitled millennials think they are? Is our method of success too good for them?" The answer is an emphatic, "No! Per chapter #1, while millennials respect BXer core values and leadership wisdom, they reject many BXer processes of growth due to the imbedded dysfunction.[23]

A model2grow: Creating growth results

Successful results are the legitimate justification for utilizing "tried and true" methods. Acknowledging that "tried and true" retention methods have produced growth and stability for decades, it's logical that BXer's would cling to their proven methods to retain their employees. It goes without saying, but who abandons successful results? However, what if the methods are no longer producing successful results? Do we hold onto them out of respect to the older generations? Do we hold onto them because that is the way we've always done it? Do we hold onto them because they were successful in the past? Or, do we allow the results to speak for themselves? If so, the "tried and true" methods of retention are not producing successful results with millennials. Actually, when we contrast the retention rates of baby boomers and genXers to the 18 months for millennials, the results of the "tried and true" methods could be defined as failure. Thus, we can respect the success of the "tried and true" methods of the past, but it's time to move on from them if we are seeking successful results.

A model2grow: Increasing 18 months

One of the most common questions I receive at my conferences is, "Why 18 months? Why are millennials moving from to job to job every 18 months?" Actually,

---

[23] Section titled, "Why do millennials reject BXer processes?

millennials are sending out resumes, CV's, and applications after 12 months. Why?

Millennials use a year to assess reality, then determine if there's an opportunity to present innovative ideas of value, or not. Is there a platform of voice, or there's not? Millennials are either heard, or they are not! It's that simple! *Voice* is the dominate factor in retention rates with millennials and the essential component to growth. The surveys reveal if there's no opportunity for *voice*, creativity, and idea development at the 12-month mark, millennials start looking elsewhere.

This is another area of heightened frustration for BXer's, who consistently state, "Who do those entitled millennials think they are, demanding a voice after just one year?" Again, millennials are not demanding a voice, millennials are leaving when there is no opportunity for voice. Per the survey results in this entire chapter, when your innovative and creative millennials consistently leave, you jeopardize your growth, forfeit profitability, disrupt fluidity, and absorb the unforeseen costs. If you are sincerely seeking to develop a model2grow and stabilize retention with millennial employees and customers, voice is an essential component of the model.

My innovative ideas of value don't matter.
See ya!

create2elevate.com
BABY BOOMER/GEN X
survey:

Does the opportunity for your employees to present their innovative ideas influence their decision to remain with your company?

YES	26%
NO	74%

+6k Participants

create2elevate.com
MILLENNIAL
survey:

Does the opportunity for you to present your innovative ideas influence your decision to remain with your company?

YES	77%
NO	23%

+22k Participants

create2elevate.com
MILLENNIAL
survey:

Does your employer value your ideas of innovation and growth?

| YES | 36% |
| NO | 64% |

+22k Participants

A model2grow: The equation of growth

Critical Assessment:
The firsthand voice in the survey reveals that nearly 8 of 10 millennials leave their job when they are convinced their innovative ideas of value will not be heard. Yet, more than 7 of 10 BXers state that the opportunity to present innovative ideas has no bearing on millennials leaving their company.
Millennial voice = millennial retention
Millennial retention = sustainable growth

After hundreds of conversations with C-Suite executives and owners, I strongly argue that the failure to see "why" millennials are leaving their company is not short sightedness, age, or pride. BXers have been raised on the ladder of success; any structure of growth outside of the ladder is foreign, which is a critical point in this research project. Understanding this reality, then utilizing the knowledge to wisely develop a path of growth WILL define your future with millennials.

If you are sincere about residing on Growth Island with millennial employees and customers, then an intentional platform of *voice* is the bridge that allows you to abandon Conflict Island for Growth Island. Empowering millennials with a *voice* is not a plank in the bridge, nor is it the foundation or the structural components that strengthen the bridge, ***voice* is the bridge!** Omitting and intentional *voice* within your structure equates to survival mode on Conflict Island; whereas, an intentional platform of *voice* for millennials equates to growth.

---

create2elevate.com
BABY BOOMER/GEN X
survey:

Is millennial retention negatively affecting your company?

YES	48%
NO	52%

+6k Participants

When I am asked to present my research to executive teams, I consistently ask the same questions throughout the presentation. One of those questions is, "What is the retention rate for your millennial employees?" Having presented the research over 100 times, not once has anyone been able to give me an answer on that day.

Actually, the most common response is given through a lens of embarrassment, "We have never tracked millennial retention rates." EVERY TIME that executive teams have followed up with me, they are stunned by the negative impact on their organization related to millennial retention rates.

Knowing that the executives take the survey prior to me presenting the research, I believe the data in this question might be skewed. Based on the follow up response and analysis of other questions in the surveys, I believe the negative impact of millennial retention exceeds 80% in all organizations.[24]

Acknowledging that "negative" is a broad term, the comprehensive research on migration in my textbook reveals that poor retention rates have three outcomes; 1) impede organizational fluidity, 2) damage morale with long-term employees, and 3) generate financial crises.[25] In other words, poor retention rates are organizational killers! However, the term "negative" possesses a deeper vein of organizational disruption with millennials.

In a world dependent upon technology, 72% of all technology jobs on the planet are currently held by millennials. That number will exceed 80% by 2020.[26] Thus, a retention issue with the employees who operate, manage, and advance the technology in your structure will disrupt your fluidity and morale at a foundational level. Millennial retention rates are not a peripheral matter; they are a foundational matter that will determine

---

[24] Question #6 in the BABY BOOMER/GEN X survey
[25] Wessinger, K. (2016). *The relationship between creative practice and socioeconomic crisis in the Caribbean: A path to sustainable growth.* Routledge: London, U.K.
[26] London School of Economics, 2017

growth and profit rates for the next two decades. Your growth depends on retaining millennials.

Case study: Voice

Last year I interviewed a 34-year-old millennial who has achieved financial and occupational success. James graduated from the University of Georgia with a bachelor's degree in information technology. Following graduation, he spent the next four years migrating from company to company seeking the "right fit" for his skill set. After four years of searching, he was hired as an analyst by a large firm in Atlanta to assess cross platform communication.

A year into the position he recognized a weakness in the company's method of assessment. Knowing that he had the ability and insight to develop a module that would clarify communication between software components, he sought permission from his boss to spend three hours per week developing a solution to the longstanding problem. His genX boss responded by saying, "I respect your desire to solve the problem; but you were hired to be an analyst, not a developer. If you maintain your excellent work ethic, you can ultimately work yourself up to a developer position." James was not satisfied with the answer, but was weary of moving from job to job.

Certain that he could solve the problem and produce a module that would benefit the company; he developed the solution on his own time. Four months later, he returned to his boss and presented the completed module. His boss respectfully and immediately rejected the module and reminded James that he had a bright future if he would remain faithful to his current role in the company. His boss then went one step further, "I am about to get promoted. I have placed your name, along with five others, in an applicant pool to interview for my position. Rocking the boat now might not be beneficial to your future." James left discouraged and determined to find another job.

Seventeen months after being hired, James left his position for a competitor who seemed to value his creative and innovative abilities. His new company recognized the value of his module, surrounded him with a collaborative team, and pitched his solution to one of their Fortune 500 clients. The client immediately purchased the module for a multi-million dollar figure and contracted with the new company to implement James' solution.

One year later, James was celebrating his 27th birthday and watching the opening of the U.S. Stock Market on CNBC. The CEO of the Fortune 500 Company that purchased James' module rung the opening bell and was subsequently interviewed. During the interview the CEO was asked, "If you could point to one decision in the last year that has strengthened your company, what is that one decision?" The CEO immediately responded by suggesting that the module that James developed allowed them to clarify their accounting methods and strengthen their market share.

That same day the stock price of the iconic Fortune 500 Company increased by over $3 per share.

The most important part of James story, James was awarded a small annual percentage of the revenue generated from the module. He took the income, purchased land in North Georgia, and built a camp for inner city kids suffering from abuse. Today, James remains a faithful and innovative employee of that company, yet he is confident that he is fulfilling his purpose by helping kids that are unable to help themselves.

Besides the obvious, there are important facts that need illuminated about James' story.

a. He migrated from job to job until his voice and ideas were respected.

b. He was not seeking his own "gig," he was determined to remain employed and secure profit for the company who employed him.

c. His employment greatly benefited the company who gave him the opportunity to develop and implement his innovation.

d. The company who quenched James' voice lost a multi-million-dollar contract, stunted their growth, and forfeited a cornerstone of sustainable profitability.

e. James was NOT interested in the next rung on the ladder. The pursuit of purpose for James meant that he was able to elevate the whole; his company, its employees, himself, family, community, and kids longing for an opportunity.

SNAPSHOT of growth:

Mission

Think of your organization and its focused mission as a bowling alley. The growth objective is to knock down all the pins at the end of the alley. You provide a clean and uninhibited lane with gutters on each side that represent your core values. Then, allow your millennial employees to collaboratively determine the most effective method to knock down the pins. Keep in mind, they may not bowl with the same motion, form, or ball spin. They might not even use a ball. But as long as they remain within your core values and achieve the focused outcome, who cares how they knocked down the pins?

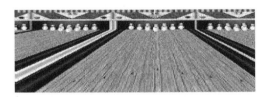

create2elevate.com
BABY BOOMER/GEN X
survey:

Is your company actively engaged in "giving back" to the local community?

Yes	68%
No	32%

+6k Participants

create2elevate.com
MILLENNIAL
survey:

Is your company actively engaged in "giving back" to the local community?

Yes	23%
No	77%

+22k Participants

A model2grow: Actively engaging

When Expert Computers in Central Georgia hired me to establish an intentional platform of voice, I was excited about the prospects of hearing innovative ideas filtered through a lens of technology. Although there were many terrific ideas that were far beyond my intellect, once again

I was reminded that millennials strategically seek to use their skillset, education, and willingness to holistically elevate the local community. The employees at Expert Computers were no different.

Based on the interaction with a local school, one of the employees recognized a profound need that was impeding the progress of the students. Although the company had donated tens of thousands of dollars of equipment to the school, the faculty needed consistent instruction regarding the technology and its rapidly changing nuances. In other words, if the faculty was limited in their knowledge of utilization of the equipment, then the students were not receiving the full benefit of the blessing.

When the idea was introduced to me as their coach, a millennial team member stated, "*Math teachers are taught to teach math, not to use the latest technology as a tool to advance their students. Actually, we have discovered that many teachers are afraid of the technology. We believe our idea can give them comfort and make them more effective teachers. Better equipped teachers produce better students and residents for our community!*" Once again, I left asking myself about millennials, "Entitled? Selfish? Lazy? I'm not seeing it!"

The details of the idea specified that each employee would spend 4 hours per week in the school providing technology instruction to teachers and/or kids that requested help. The group proposed that the company give each employee two paid hours per week to be actively engaged in the school; in return the employee would also give two hours of their own time; a total of 4 hours per employee in the school.

My initial thought when the group first presented me the idea; "Wow! No matter the size of the company or the location of the community, millennials see life through a holistic lens. Their idea collaboratively elevates the employees, customers, company AND the community as a whole." Furthermore, after hearing the idea, I responded with one question, *"What made you pick this idea?"* The response, *"We like this idea because it is perfectly aligned with the company's core values. We have 12 core values and it directly relates to every one of them."*

I would be remiss, as a baby boomer, if I did not propose this question, *Is there anything in their idea that screams or insinuates entitled, lazy, or selfish?* In the spirit of transparency, after hearing hundreds of ideas from create2elevate events, the most selfish ideas seem to be generated by baby boomers and genX. However, I have witnessed an undeniable pattern of holistic ideas generated from millennials.

As a non-millennial leader, you may be asking, "Community driven ideas are terrific, but how do they help me fortify growth and profitability?" At the create2elevate events, the ideas generated, presented, and selected for implementation relate specifically to products and processes of growth and profit. However, every event we've led has had at least one holistically driven idea selected and implemented.

How are holistic ideas profitable? If I have done my job presenting the research, you know by now the significance of a platform of voice as it relates to retention of employees and talent acquisition. It is those same employees who provide fluidity, stability, and growth; all of which equate to profitability. However, building holistic capital in your community or communities that you represent, endears your brand, products, and/or service to millennial customers.

create2elevate.com
BABY BOOMER/GEN X
survey:

Does having the opportunity to "give back" to your local community through active engagement factor into your decision to remain with your current company?

Yes	17%
No	83%

+6k Participants

create2elevate.com
MILLENNIAL
survey:

Does having the opportunity to "give back" to your local community through active engagement factor into your decision to remain with your current company?

Yes	76%
No	24%

+22k Participants

Critical Assessment:

Holistic capital heavily influences retention rates, talent acquisition, and customer base. In order to secure sustainable growth and profitability with millennial employees and customers, holistic capital will be a factor that could seal the fate of your company.

While 76% of millennials state that "giving back" through active engagement in the local community is a determining factor of remaining on their job, only 17% of BXers indicate that "giving back" is a reason to remain; revealing another clash of perspective that has produced cloudy waters in a beautiful environment of sacrifice. Unfortunately, the paradigm shift in perspective has defined the conflict between BXers and millennials. BXers legitimately want millennial employees to be fully focused on the company's objectives; whereas millennials desire for the objectives to be inclusive of holistic community engagement. Isn't it possible to have both?

Based on the millennial perspective of "active engagement," if managed wisely, it seems that corporations, organizations, and nations are in a win-win position.

A model2grow: Growing the millennial way

Strategic and active engagement in the lives of hurting, sick, and marginalized people is a beautiful expression of the most powerful force known to humanity...love. The generations preceding millennials have been the most generous generations in history, donating billions of dollars to fund and establish charitable institutions that positively affect the outcomes of many lives throughout the world. Whereas, millennials respect and revere the sacrifices made to help people, the surveys reveal that millennials are redefining "active engagement" with charitable causes and organizations. While one definition of "active engagement" is pushing out, the other is pushing in; creating a cumbersome cross current that must be wisely managed. If the cross currents are misjudged, the outcome could be deadly to organizational structures and thus, forfeiting the opportunity for growth with millennial employees and customers.

The majority of BXers define "actively" as a financial investment into worthy and just causes in the local community, I.e.: Writing a check. Millennials define "actively" as the hands-on engagement of elevating the health, environment, and residents in the local community. One perspective of "active engagement" funds an agency to save people, while the other perspective chooses to physically rescue them. Neither perspective is wrong, and both perspectives have elevated the lives of many; however, the surveys reveal that facilitating "active engagement" in the local community is essential to retention, talent acquisition, and growth with millennials.

Daymond John, founder of FUBU and investor on Shark Tank says, *"You are not born a winner, you are not born a loser, you ARE born a chooser!"* Millennials are choosing a holistic way of growth and success. Millennials are resolutely choosing to work, lead, parent, eat, worship, exercise, vacation, and grow holistically. In lieu of measuring success with the density of accumulation, millennials are choosing to insulate their lives, companies who employee them, children they parent, and communities they live in with layers of holistic wellbeing.

Ironically, as judgment continues to spew like an active volcano toward millennials, they choose to use the knowledge gained from the front row to save BXer companies, grandchildren, and nations from the debilitating outcomes from the ladder of success. Thus, millennials have concluded that the only way to reach the holistic health found on Growth Island is to leave the toxicity behind on Conflict Island, which is to reject the

BXer ladder of success for the prospects of a healthy whole.

Although the financial security and achievement on Conflict Island is unparalleled and respected, millennials are passionate about leaving behind the impediments that threaten sustainable growth of companies, families, communities, and nations.

Holistic Capital

A collaborative and accumulated asset measured by the breadth of good will.

Growth tool: Fortify growth by building your holistic capital

A model2grow: Holistic capital

You can measure your holistic capital by answering two questions:

1. Are you actively elevating the whole? Not just writing checks, but leaving your thumbprint of a committed and loving sacrifice on people and the environment?

2. How full is your bucket of accumulation?

A model2grow: Where and How?

To the surprise of millennials, I hear very little complaint from C-Suite executives or management teams regarding the inclusion of community engagement in the company's objectives. The question is, "How and where to engage while remaining focused on fulfilling the responsibilities of the job with the company." This is another reason why the platform of voice is crucial to your growth.

Stop fretting over the decisions required to develop productive ideas. Turn the table of idea generation over to your employees through an intentional platform of voice. Allow your employees to develop, compete, and present their ideas of how and where.

A model2grow: Why not?

The create2elevate research lab that I founded in 2015 has been successfully developing platforms of voice in governments, corporations, organizations, and houses of worship in the United States, Caribbean, and Central America. The strategic objectives of the create2elevate platform of voice is to solidify retention, hone talent acquisition, generate innovative ideas of value, secure growth, and fortify profitability.[27] The two-month coaching process culminates with an event where teams competitively present their innovative ideas of value. Every event that we've led has had a minimum of 3-4 groups who presented ideas that were holistically driven.

---

[27] If interested in having the create2elevate team establish a platform of voice in your organization, please contact me at kent@create2elevate.com

A model2grow: Empty the bucket

As a 12-year-old kid sitting on the back porch of my grandparents' home in North Atlanta in the 1970's, I remember seeing my tough grandfather who fought in World War II tear up. When I asked him what was wrong, he said, "Pete kicked the bucket." Pete was my grandfather's beloved bird dog, and he had just died.

For over a century, the phrase, "kick the bucket" unquestionably stood for death, but with a few strokes on the keyboard Justin Zackham transformed a long-held symbolism of death into a worldwide symbol of life.[28] Today, when someone says, "my bucket list," there is no doubt that the conversation is focused on beautiful and adventurous experiences of life.

As the cultural transformation continues to evolve for the bucket, the kind and quantity of the experiences placed in the bucket has become a measure of success. The objective is to fill the bucket with experiential achievement prior to "kicking the bucket." The fuller the bucket at the end of life indicates the greater the life was when lived.

The data from the millennial survey indicates that millennials view the "bucket list" through a different lens of perspective than BXers. The millennial lens is steeped in holistic purpose, while the BXer lens is defined by personal experience. Nearly 7 of 10 millennials state that they are filling their buckets with adventures related to environmental causes, feeding the poor, organizing co-ops, joining the Peace Corp, and taking mission trips. Conversely, the BXer buckets are being filled with

---

[28] Justin Zackman: www.imdb.com (2019).

personal adventures; like Alaskan cruises, trips to Italy, and exotic Caribbean destinations.

There is one more interesting observation regarding the buckets. While BXers seek to fill their bucket with personal experiences, millennials are emptying their buckets in an effort to elevate others. Millennials are utilizing their personal resources to fund adventures that pour out sacrifice, love, and compassion on marginalized people.

Since there is nothing wrong with vacations or spending hard earned resources on rest, why are millennials breaking from tradition and using their vacation time to elevate marginalized people? Millennials recognize that struggling communities cannot be transformed to healthy communities through checked lists in full buckets. Furthermore, millennials measure personal security through the holistic health of community, whereas BXers seem to measure personal security by the density of accumulation.[29]

An empty bucket does not imply financial despair; it indicates a mission of holistic health. Millennials define growth through empty buckets.

---

[29] Refer to Chapter #1, A lens2understand, section titled, *Identity*

You decide?

Based on the contents in each bucket, who benefits?

BXer Bucket:
- Another box checked on the list
- Personal experiential adventure
- Self-elevating
- Social "Standing" capital

Millennial Bucket:
- Relationship with a family in another culture (I.e.: AirBnB)
- Experiential adventure to help others
- Active engagement in community and environmental causes
- Holistic capital

create2elevate.com
MILLENNIAL
survey:

Do you measure your occupational achievement through company profit or fulfillment of purpose?

Purpose   73%
Profit   27%

+22k participants

A model2grow: Align purpose to get profit

The emphatic information coming from 82% millennials in the profit vs. purpose question is, "We have a purpose and we will achieve it! Even if it means we must migrate from job to job to job until we find a company willing to provide the opportunity." Make no mistake; fulfilling purpose for millennials is personal and nonnegotiable. Employers who have stifled purpose with their insistence of climbing the ladder of success have lost innovators of growth and forfeited profit. Yet, developing an environment that facilitates "purpose" is essential to talent attraction and product relevance to millennial customers. Companies who allow and align millennial employees to fulfill purpose are securing profit through extraordinary expansion and innovative growth.

77

!

ATTN: ALL BABY BOOMERS AND GENERATION X

Millennials are <u>mission</u> driven!

Coincidence?

Applications for the U.S. Peace Corp are at a 40-year high.

peacecorp.gov, 2017

ATTN: Long tenured BXer employees

Why are you threatened by millennial employees?

Although long-term employees do not use the word "threat," the venom flowing from tenured BXer employees toward millennials indicates a bitter conflict steeped in threat. There is NO need to be threatened by millennials, they do not want to take your job, be your competition, put you out of business, nor climb your ladder of success. They seek the same growth objective that you seek. Millennials define work as a collaborative process, grow the company through innovative ideas, satisfy purpose, establish relevancy, and ownership of process. That reality is a win-win for everyone!

A model2grow: A secure and complete model

Let's apply sound logic, based from the data in the surveys, to ensure a secure and complete model of growth. If you take the step to provide an intentional platform of voice for employees to present their innovative ideas of value; the outcomes are as follows:
1. Millennial retention rates stabilize,
2. The "negative" impact on your organization will be transformed to positive,
3. Profit will increase since it's not being forfeited on an escalating onboarding, training, and lost productivity,
4. Ideas presented and implemented will become your cornerstones of sustainable growth and profitability.

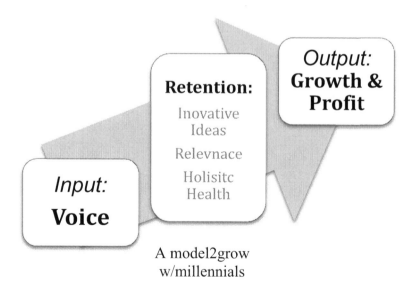

A model2grow
w/millennials

Model-NOT-2grow: A punch in the gut

I am thankful that many of my clients use me to strengthen their relationships with their top customers. The events are typically held in hotel ballrooms, conference centers, or universities. My objective is to equip leaders with the tools to secure growth and fortify profitability with millennial employees and customers. My clients recognize the reciprocal value of the events; if they ensure growth for their customers, they ensure growth for themselves.

Each of the events provide me with the privilege of meeting some of the most astute and successful leaders in the corporate community. One of those leaders was the President of a well-known wealth management company. Several months after the event he requested that I meet with him and his Board of Directors. As part of his introduction, he made the following statement, "While I was driving home from Dr. Wessinger's research presentation in Tampa 2 months ago, one of his cost analysis realities punched me in the gut! While we are focused on the cost associated with supplies in our break rooms, travel expense, and marketing, there is an unaccounted expenditure hiding in the back room. This expenditure is stealing our profit and impeding growth! He's about to break it down for you."

Great leaders always factor cost. The data from the survey shows that replacing one millennial employee comes at a high cost. Question #8 in the NON-millennial survey states, "How much does it cost to replace one millennial employee?" Noting that the number one answer is $30k-$40k, 11% of the respondent's state that it cost their company over $50k to replace one millennial employee. That means that 43% of the respondents state they expend more than $30k to replace one millennial employee. That is a staggering figure, but we cannot be guilty of omitting the most important variable in the equation. Retention greatly impacts trajectories of growth and profitability.

Let's conservatively select $35k as the median cost to replace one employee. If we apply that figure to a baby boomer, the $35k is factored out over the retention rate of 19.1 years. That equates to an annual expenditure of $1,832 per year. When we apply the same figure to genX, who's retention rate is 9.2 years, we have an annual expense of $3,804. However, when we apply the $35k figure to millennials, who's retention rate is 18 months, the annual expenditure is $23,333! Retention matters!

Further, what line item does that expenditure come from in your budget? No matter the line item, we know for certain that the cost negatively affects growth and profit. If we are not retaining our millennial employees, we are forfeiting profit and destabilizing our growth.

create2elevate.com
BABY BOOMER/GEN X
survey:

What does it cost to replace one millennial employee?

$30K - $40K	**32%**
Less than $10K	24%
$10k - $20k	19%
$20k - $30K	14%
Greater than $50k	11%

+6k Participants

Model-NOT-2grow: Appeasing millennials with token bridges

One of my largest clients is BB&T Bank. After seeing the outcomes of this research project, they astutely formed a millennial engagement team and provided them with a platform of voice. The leadership of the bank asked me to oversee their first meeting. Before we began, I gave the group of 27 millennials guidelines for the meeting. In our quest to improve employee retention and secure relevancy with a millennial customer base, we gave them the freedom to speak plainly about anything related to structure, marketing, and/or process.

Within 30 seconds, a millennial sitting next to me said, "I'll go first. Whoever is tweeting for the bank, please stop! It's embarrassing and not productive. It's making all the boomers and genX feel good, but millennials are laughing their ass off. In your attempt to get millennials customers, it feels like you are appeasing them by tweeting goofy messages. It's not working!"

Let me remind you again of our objective, secure growth and fortify profit with millennial employees and customers. Remaining in the cost analysis mindset from the previous section, let's talk about how appeasing millennials can also be expensive.

Token bridges that lead to "nowhere" are expensive and emphatically communicate a message to employees—neither you or your innovative ideas of value matter.

Case Study: Token Bridges

I lived on the island of St. John in the United States Virgin Islands for a decade. The majestic island is only accessible by boat, which means that tourists must land at the St. Thomas airport and catch a taxi to the ferry that takes them to St. John.

The quickest and most efficient route to the St. John ferry from the St Thomas airport goes through a coastal region called Bovoni. Due to tidal changes and storm swells, flooding is a frequent issue at a pivotal intersection in the heart of Bovoni. The water level regularly rises above the road and prevents passage, which prohibits tourists from reaching their scheduled ferry to St. John. As a result, the taxi drivers are forced to take an alternative route to the St. John ferry. The route requires the drivers to navigate an extreme mountainous terrain and travel nearly twice the distance. The travel time reduces the number of trips that a driver can take per day, while the rugged terrain exponentially elevates maintenance costs on the taxis.

When the tourists fail to reach their ferry, blame spews like a broken dam. Angry tourists suffering from motion sickness blame the taxi drivers who "took the long way," fuming taxi drivers blame the government for not providing an efficient route, and the proprietors in St. John blame the dysfunction on everyone in St Thomas.

Although St. Thomas offers an extraordinary product with the world's most beautiful beaches, stunning mountain views of the Caribbean, and world-class shopping; the inability to progressively modernize the transportation process has given their competitors an economic advantage. Other islands, such as Jamaica, have intently listened to the voice of their employees and built innovative road systems that allow their customers to flow without impediments.

Case Study: **Who has the solution?**

Due to the daily routine of transporting and interacting with their customers, the taxi drivers are certain they have a solution that will ease the tension on Conflict Island, which would retain customers and secure growth for decades to come. The taxi drivers recognize that a short bridge over one frequently flooded intersection would reduce the travel time to the ferry by 30 minutes. The reduction in time would ensure tourists that they would always be on time for their ferry, allow the taxi drivers to earn twice the money due to the increase in number of trips per day, and reduce vehicle maintenance costs significantly. A bridge would be a "win" for everyone.

Ignoring the voice of innovation, the inaction of the political leaders intensified the conflict and negatively influenced the attitude, productivity, and morale of the most important people in the process of growth. To justify the exclusion, the political leaders inadvertently valued the strength of their product over the people who made the product viable. The taxi drivers are the first face, first impression, first voice, first ear, last impression, last ear, and last voice for every tourist that visits St. John. However, the political leaders valued the aquamarine waters, tropical terrain, and the exquisite villas above the first face, impression, ear, and voice representing their product.

Falsely assuming that the product was the strength of their business, the voice and perspective of the taxi drivers was ignored based on a gap in perspective, "The taxi drivers need to pay their dues just like we had to pay our dues. This is the way it's always been done and we're not changing our successful process just to make those "entitled" taxi drivers happy!" In other words, "pay your dues, climb our ladder, and one day you will be privileged to sit in our seat of leadership."

Case Study: Ignored "voice" of innovation

The delivery of tourists (customers) to St. John is essential for growth and profit; therefore, the "entitled" taxi drivers are the most critical piece of the growth process. If taxi drivers are impeded or prohibited from preforming their task at the most proficient level, the entire process of growth breaks down and profitability is forfeited. The taxi drivers are the key to sustainable growth and profit.

    Frustrated that their solution of a shorter and more efficient route is ignored, many of the best taxi drivers grew weary of the conflict and left for other positions. As a result, the taxi driver retention rate negatively affected the quality of the product, impeded the process of growth, and compromised sustainable profit. Make no mistake; the taxi driver retention rates that threaten sustainable growth are directly linked to the ignored voice of the taxi drivers; when the voice of innovation is ignored, retention plummets, and sustainable growth is jeopardized.

Case Study: Reaching for Growth Island

Recognizing that the strategy to quench the voice of the drivers through the status quo had failed, the Virgin Islands government responded to the taxi driver retention issue and the imminent threat to growth by wisely constructing a beautiful bridge adjacent to the current road. When the bridge was completed the business owners on St. John, taxi drivers on St. Thomas, and residents of the two islands all applauded the government for solving the conflict that suppressed growth. Celebrating their accomplishment, the Virgin Islands government indicated that the comprehensive planning period, immense expense, and lengthy inconvenience in building the bridge was all justified for three reasons; 1) to retain taxi drivers, 2) ease the travel burden for tourists, and 3) secure growth. Further, government leaders solidified the legacy of their leadership by finally listening to the "entitled" taxi drivers and securing a profitable solution.[30] Or did they?

Case Study: Bridges define the legacy of your leadership

Twenty years after the bridge was completed, the bridge has never been connected to the adjacent road. Although the bridge has endured the destructive force of hurricanes, tumultuous threats from sea currents, and sweltering sun of the Caribbean; "The Bridge to Nowhere" remains a frustrating reminder that the bridge alone did not solve the problem.

Today, taxi drivers are still forced to take the long route through the mountainous terrain, tourists miss their scheduled ferries, conflict remains a permanent portrait at the ferry dock, and the retention rate of taxi drivers is a debilitating reality.

---

[30] Correlation: Taxi drivers = employees; Government leaders = Organizational management; Tourists = customers.

If you passed by the bridge today, you would see a small white plastic table and four plastic chairs sitting in the middle of the bridge. Each evening older men gather on the bridge to play a friendly game of dominos. I call it the most expensive domino table in the world!

Although the solution to the flooding crisis seemed to be unquestionably correct, tens of millions of dollars were spent to solve a problem that is nothing more than a game table and a monument of faulty leadership.

The question becomes, "Why would they spend so money building a bridge, if they knew they were not going to connect to the road? After speaking directly to four top level government leaders, including the Prime Minister, their intention was always to connect the bridge to the road. However, after 23 years, each government official told me, "It has not been a fiscal priority."

Every time a resident or tourist drives by the "Bridge to Nowhere," the first thought is, "Wow! That is an example of bad leadership." Yet, every time a former taxi driver travels by the bridge, they must be thinking, "If the 'powers at be' would have listened, what could have been?"

Case Study: **Bridges communicate intention**

Throughout the 3-year construction of the bridge, the taxi drivers felt as if their voice was heard and innovative ideas respected, which infused their attitude with value and elevated retention. Further, the construction of the bridge communicated to the tourists that the loyalty to their brand was sincerely appreciated. However, did the token bridge secure growth through employee and customer retention? Actually, the failure to connect the bridge to the road of growth plummeted taxi driver retention rates and pushed tourists to other islands vying for their money.

Everyone longs for a bridge to Growth Island, but token bridges to "Nowhere" inflate conflict with those who matter most, suppress their innovative ideas of value, and deepen economic crisis. Again, token bridges that lead to "nowhere" are expensive and emphatically communicate a message to employees—neither you or your innovative ideas of value matter.

STOP!

In an effort to appease millennials "until the storm blows over," what percentage of your balance sheet is consumed by the expense of building token bridges to "Nowhere?"

How much money is spent to fund activity on token bridges to "Nowhere?"

The firsthand voice in the surveys reveals that the path to sustainable growth and profit is secured by building a bridge to Growth Island. Resist the temptation of building expensive bridges to "nowhere" in an effort to temporarily appease millennials. Only build bridges that produce outcomes of sustainable growth and profitability WITH millennial employees and customers.

Substance OR Rhetoric?

BREAKING NEWS …. Legislated equality has been an expense failure!

A reality that I did not foresee in the outcomes of this project was the reality of equality. When employees get the opportunity to present their innovative ideas of value, those who are assessing and rewarding those ideas are typically the C-Suite execs or the management team. Every employee that stands on the stage suddenly realizes that their voice matters, and their ideas are equally respected. Further, when the top ideas are rewarded; race, gender, religion, ethnicity, age, seniority, or position are never a factor. Great ideas are great ideas, irrespective of who is presenting them! Level the playing in your company by creating a platform of voice for ALL employees to present their innovative ideas of value. Innovative ideas that secure sustainable growth is void of race, gender, religion, and ethnicity.

Prove to your employees and customers that you're serious about establishing an environment that respects all people.

Platform of voice = Equality

Millennials reject what?

BXer **METHOD** to financial success....

One rung at a time!

BXer **DEFINITION** of success

Accumulate a full bucket

Why worry about a future with millennials ... when you can create one!

The key terms are, *"You, create, and future."* <u>You</u> have the opportunity to <u>create</u> an extraordinary <u>future</u> with millennial employees, members, and customers. Although the structure for growth may not emulate the past, your future with millennials can be the greatest era of growth your organization has ever known.

-OR-

CHAPTER REVIEW: A model2grow w/ millennial employees

- The model2grow:
  Millennial voice = millennial retention;
  Millennial retention = sustainable growth.
  Reminder; millennial voice generates innovative
  ideas of value, which are cornerstones of growth.

- Growth and profitability are dependent on
  millennial employee retention, yet millennial
  retention is dependent upon a respected *voice*.

- Millennials are not demanding a *voice*, millennials
  are leaving when there is no opportunity for *voice*.

- Longstanding "tried and true" methods of
  retention seem to be rooted in an unshakable
  trajectory of growth, millennials continue to
  migrate from job to job at a higher rate than any
  other demographic ever recorded

- The "tried and true" methods of retention are not
  producing successful results with millennials.

- Millennial retention rates are not a peripheral
  matter; they are a foundational matter that will
  determine growth and profit rates for the next two
  decades.

- Facilitating "active engagement" in the local
  community is essential to retention, talent
  acquisition, and growth with millennials.

- Millennials define growth through empty buckets.
- The data from the survey shows that replacing one millennial employee comes at a high cost.

- Token bridges that lead to "nowhere" are expensive and emphatically communicate a message to employees—neither you or your innovative ideas of value matter.

"The only way to generate enduring profits is to begin by building the kind of work environment that attracts, focuses, and keeps talented employees."
Buckingham, M. & Coffman C. (1999)[31]

---

[31] Buckingham, M. & Coffman C. (1999). *First, break all the rules.* Simon & Schuster; New York, NY

Chapter 3

strategy2profit

w/ millennial customers

Does your organization have a strategy to reach millennial customers?

BEFORE *you turn the page and assess the results of the surveys ... be prepared to focus on the contrast between the answers from the baby boomer/Gen X and millennial surveys.*

create2elevate.com
BABY BOOMER/GEN X
survey:

Is your organization's marketing and product line relevant to millennials?

YES	57%
NO	43%

+6k Participants

create2elevate.com
MILLENNIAL
survey:

Is your employer's marketing and product line relevant to millennials?

YES	28%
NO	72%

+22k Participants

97

create2elevate.com
BABY BOOMER/GEN X
survey:

Does your organization have a strategy to reach millennial customers?

YES   51%
NO   49%

+6k Participants

create2elevate.com
MILLENNIAL
survey:

Does your employer have a strategy to reach millennial customers?

YES   26%
NO   74%

+22k Participants

Critical Assessment:

Transfer of wealth, purchasing power, and population size should merit a precise and intentional strategy to reach millennial customers; yet, by their own admission, 51% of BXers state they have NO strategy to reach millennial customers, while 57% state their marketing and product line is NOT relevant to millennial customers. Millennials indicate that the situation is far worse than BXers suggest. They state that 72% do not have a relevant product line and marketing strategy, and 74% do not have a strategy to reach millennial customers. The analysis would indicate that those BXer leaders either have their head in the sand, ignorant to reality, or suffer from poor leadership skills. Either way, their respective organizations are not positioned to grow or profit.

A strategy2profit: Seal your fate

Following my research presentation in the historic port city of Savannah, Georgia, a millennial named Sofia in her early thirties hastily approached me with her story of growth and profit. She was employed by a regional bank in a saturated real estate market in middle Georgia. Struggling to survive and contemplating a career change, she asked her herself, "Where do I want to live and what type of house do I want live in?" She strongly felt if she could answer those questions as a "raging millennial," that she could grow an untapped market and grow her career.

Her answers became her model2grow and strategy2profit; an 800 square foot house within walking distance to town, low debt, green building materials, and alternative energy sources. She took a risk and developed the first one on her own, before it was completed it was sold to a millennial couple. Within 18 months she had built and closed on 31 houses that sold for less than $50k, all financed by the bank who employed her. In lieu of focusing on the ineffective "tried and true" methods of mortgage banking, she formulated an intentional strategy to reach the millennial customer base with a product line that she knew was relevant. As a result, she secured growth and fortified profit for herself and her employer.

create2elevate.com
MILLENNIAL
survey:

Does your company provide an environment to formally present your ideas of innovation and growth?

YES	32%
NO	68%

+22k Participants

Critical Assessment:
Based on the firsthand voice in this project, the answer to this question will determine if your organization is positioned to grow in profit or die in crisis. The millennial voice in this question states that only 3 of 10 (32%) are positioned to grow, while 7 of 10 (68%) companies are increasingly becoming irrelevant and on a path of death.

A strategy2profit: Focus on relevancy

This question is NOT about retention; it is unequivocally about *relevancy* to your customer base. Are you effectively utilizing your millennial employees to secure growth with millennial customers? No matter your answer, this chapter will equip you with a strategy, tools, and methods to profit with a millennial customer base through your millennial employees.

Irrespective of the size, scale, or strength of your product, the outcomes of your future are dependent on the innovative ideas generated by your millennial employees. Yet, the surveys show another layer of conflict that could potentially derail growth and forfeit volumes of profit. While +22k millennials state there is rarely an environment to present their innovative ideas, 6 of 10 BXers believe there is such an environment.

The analysis of the contrast indicates that millennials and BXers define the term "environment" differently. While millennials are seeking an intentional and formal environment that is focused on idea development, BXers seem to define "environment" as an idea box or random questions in a staff meeting. Both of the BXer expressions communicate a demeaning message, that ideas of substance are only generated at the top levels of the organizational structure. Actually, BXers admit to this reality in the survey.

create2elevate.com
BABY BOOMER/GEN X
survey:

Who is the source of innovative ideas in your company?

Owner	17%
Management	79%
Other employees	4%

+6k Participants

A strategy2profit: Determine who is the source of relevancy

Who is the source of innovation in your organizational structure? Who is the first face, first voice, and first ear that your customers engage? Is it the owner? Is it management? Or is it other? If the "other" employees have the ear of your customers, wouldn't the "other" understand the customer's needs and desires more than those in the top of the tower?[32]

I want to challenge BXers to interpret the 4%, who are they? Per the BXer voice in the survey, it seems that 96% of innovation is generated from those on the BXer ladder of success, which is to be commended as a profitable model of growth for many generations. However, who is the "other?" What demographic is represented in the "other?" What percentage of your employee base is not owner or management? Does the "other" have innovative ideas of value that could become the cornerstones of growth for the next two decades? How do you know unless you provide a platform of voice?

Please forgive the repetition, but to understand "Why" your future is dependent upon the innovative ideas of your millennial employees, or can I say the 4%, please note that no one understands millennials like millennials. If BXers ignore or omit the innovative ideas from millennial employees, they will lose relevance to the

---

[32] When the create2elevate research lab is hired to establish a platform of voice, we conduct a pre-event, mid-event, and post-event employment assessment throughout the organization. One of the questions in the assessment is, "Who is the source of innovative ideas within the company?" In all the organizations with 50 or fewer employees, the top answer is consistently the owner, which explains why the growth potential has been limited.

customer base that possesses the largest annual purchasing power ever recorded and recipients of the greatest transfer of wealth in the history of humanity. If BXers fail to provide a platform of voice to generate innovative ideas from millennial employees, they will seal the fate of financial crisis and organizational death. However, if BXers provide a platform of voice, they are sealing a fate of sustainable growth and profit. For those leaders who are willing to build a bridge of growth to millennials, the opportunity for profit has never been so ripe.

SNAPSHOT of profit:

Talent Acquisition

If your source of innovation emulates the BXer voice in the survey, a loud and defining message is being sent to all potential employees. The message…your voice, ideas, and innovative potential do not matter until you climb the rungs on our ladder of success.

One of the top questions I receive at my conferences, "Why are we struggling to recruit millennials for entry level positions?" My reply consistently comes from the voice of millennials in the surveys, "Are you providing and promoting a platform of voice for millennials to articulate their innovative ideas of value? Or, are you promoting your ladder of success?" If your method to generate innovation is 96% management and owners, who wants to join the 4%? The answer, not the employees you want!

Employees = Relevancy, Relevancy = Profit

A strategy2profit: Put away fear

Knowing the millennial "issue" permeates and affects every sector of business and community, I am consistently approached by BXers wanting to have a conversation about millennials. Most of the conversations are rooted in either naivety, arrogance, or ignorance. The arrogant see themselves and their career as superior to millennials, while the ignorant are steeped in judgement; I.e.: "Those damn millennials …" However, both positions share some naive common denominators, they assume their organizations are relevant to millennials and understand the millennial perspectives. Second, they use their arrogance or ignorance to cover up one reality; internally they are fearful that they do not know how to solve the relevancy problem. For several decades BXers have been the problem solvers, which is a reality that is hard to let go. The data shows that BXers not only need to let go, but must put away fear and allow millennials to solve the problem of relevance. Again, no one knows the millennial customer base like millennial employees. No one knows what's relevant to millennial customers, like millennial employees.

A strategy2profit: Use firm footing

Living in "paradise" means you have a constant flow of family, friends, and "wannabe friends" seeking "sun and fun" on a shoe-string budget. After leading a school in Jamaica for several years, I made the decision to capitalize on the lure of "paradise" by recruiting groups of youth from the United States and Canada to visit our school throughout the summer. However, their objective reached beyond white sand beaches, clear aquamarine waters, and fish filled coral reefs; their mission was to

105

improve the everyday lives of people isolated in rural communities. The groups painted houses, built churches, cleaned schools, and many other extraordinary sacrifices of love and acceptance.

After serving people for 5 days in remote villages, we would cap off the week indulging on "paradise" in the seaside town of Ocho Rios. The most requested destination was the beautiful Dunn's River Falls. The waterway is a marvel of God; a spectacular winding river flowing from layers of mountains in the backdrop, bordered with lush tropical flora emanating the love languages of magnificent exotic birds. Just before the elevated river pours into the Caribbean Sea, the river drops through a series of tall jagged stone cliffs. Most visitors cannot resist the temptation to climb the face of the cliffs, while the pure mountain water showers them with cool expressions of paradise.

Oddly, lodged in the mouth of bliss is a deceptive reality that defies logic. As the water from the river spills into the Caribbean Sea, both the river and the sea are incredibly clear, giving the impression that when the two collide there will be a euphoric dance of nature in paradise. However, the reality is just the opposite; the visibility where the two majestic waters meet is cloudy, turbulent, and dangerous.

When the force of the river collides with the mightiest natural force on Earth, it would seem that the colossal force of the sea would ruthlessly conquer the river without ever suffering a defeat; yet the river proves to be a formable foe. While the sea is demonstrating its force through relentless waves disrupting the white sands on both sides of the mouth of the river, the river has command over its domain. Several hundred feet wide and a mile out from the island, the top water belongs to the river and its currents, while the bottom water and its currents belong to the sea. The top five feet of the cloudy turbulent water is forcibly pushing out to the open sea, while the undercurrent on the bottom is pressing toward the shoreline; making these waters extremely dangerous.

As I was sitting on the beach waiting for one of our groups to come down from the falls, I noticed a father and son from the group walk out into the sea for a swim. They weren't great swimmers, but they were celebrating an amazing week of fulfillment and bonding in paradise.

Looking back to the falls for others in the group, I took my eye off the father and son in the sea for a brief moment. When I turned back around, I was instantly concerned. They had unassumingly swam into the river currents and were quickly being pushed out to sea. Panicked by their reality, they began to swim as hard as they could back toward the shoreline, but they were no match for the strong river currents. I immediately jumped into the currents and swam out to them, when I reached them, they had already exhausted their energy and were in a deep state of fright. Although they were fearful about being swept out to open sea, I was more fearful they would get sucked down into the undercurrent and drown.

In their panicked mode to survive, they thrust themselves onto me for help. Knowing that their fear was going to get all of us killed if they did not let go, I forced the dad off me, held onto the son, and told the dad to follow me. Instead of swimming toward the shoreline or out to sea, we swam parallel to the shoreline and quickly made it to safe waters that allowed us to walk on the bottom back to the beach.

In their frantic desire to survive, their instinct said swim toward the island, but in an act that defied their instinct, they were shocked to discover that waist deep waters were only 30 feet away. Misjudging currents can be deadly.

As a reminder from Chapter 2, **change is not growth and rarely makes a difference**.[33] Let's dig deeper into that reality. When organizations attempt to save themselves from fierce currents, I.e.: Millennials, they typically seek change through one of two natural responses; swim with or against the current. Both have enormous implications on the future of the organization.

Swimming with the current is easy and seems fluid, a path of least resistance. However, swimming with the current has a destination of demise. After the realization of being swept far out to sea becomes a reality, the organization legitimately panics, reverses course, and attempts to swim back to safety; but the organization has drifted too far from shore and drowns in exhaustion.

Tragically, the other natural response has the same outcome. A resolute decision to swim against the current, which in our context is to consciously reject the innovative insights of millennials, has a trajectory of exhaustion, panic, and drowning.

Following a research presentation in a historic North Carolina city, the city manager and HR Director requested an "urgent" meeting to discuss millennial retention from a municipality perspective. Noting that both were born and raised in the area, they were legitimately proud of their city and its' 200 years of history. Marked by well-traveled cobble stone streets, towering marble statutes, majestic oak trees that lined

---

[33] Refer to Chapter 2, section titled; A model2grow: Change is not growth

main street, rows of mom and pop boutiques, and a vaudeville theater that had hosted legends like Charlie Chaplin, Clark Gable, and Charlton Heston; everything about the city seemed like a dream city. It's no wonder why 100's of movies use the backdrop of the downtown district to recapture the splendor of small-town culture in America. Yet, the reality is that the beautiful historic city is on life support and rapidly approaching death.

Due to the migration of millennial residents to Charlotte, Atlanta, Ashville, and Charleston; they informed me that within 15 years the city would be a desolate symbol of inaction. Knowing the only hope of survival was to retain and attract millennial residents, they scheduled me to speak to the entire 20-member city council. After presenting the research, as I always do, I opened the floor for questions. Without hesitation, the Head of Public Works, who sat next to me, raised his hand and said, "I have a comment to make, I don't give a damn what those fucking millennials want!" He stood to his feet and walked out of the room. As the room sat in an awkward and shocked silence, the Mayor spoke up, "We just witnessed why we are dying! The choice is ours, grow or die."

Although the response from the Department Head validated key components in the research, I took some time to critically assess his response. Why would he so quickly jump to the extreme position of rejection? He viewed millennials as a threat, not to his occupational position, but to his sphere of reality. He was no different than the guys drowning when they misjudged the cross currents. When he recognized that the strong currents associated with millennials were pushing him further away from his security, he panicked. His security was his historic city, the only city that he knew. The city that he had devoted his entire life. Like the guys drowning in the cross currents, he could only process two views, the one in front of him and the behind him. The one in front was the open sea with no land in sight, but the one behind was his security, his place of familiarity. He looked back and saw a majestic beauty and was resolutely determined not to let go; however, he failed to recognize that he was living on Conflict Island. An island that was sinking into the sea.

In both cases, panic mode was engaged, one sought my assistance and guidance based on data acquired, the other rejected. One was saved, the other is still drowning in crisis. Although my guidance seems incongruent and irrational, the research emphatically indicates that neither of the natural responses will result in growth. Actually, they both result in death.

If your response is to look back, remaining steadfast to the "tried and true" methods of the past, the currents are too strong you. You will drown in exhaustion trying to reach your glorious reality. If you've decided to take the currents out to sea, hoping for a fresh new reality, you will also drown in exhaustion trying to reach a place that does not exist.

No matter whether we resist or embrace change, growth and change are perpendicular realities. Change is a futile horizontal movement, while growth vertically elevates the entire organization. BXers must choose, growth or change? The natural response is change, but security is not found in change, it is found in the footing just 30 feet away. However, to reach it, you must be prepared to deny your visual instinct, trust the data, and move perpendicularly.

I know this is hard for many BXers to swallow, but the innovative ideas of value from millennials can save you from drowning! Your firm footing is a platform of voice, and it's just a bridge away from where you currently reside. Giving a voice to millennials is not natural, but will prove to be very profitable.

Millennials are seeking growth and requesting a voice at the table to create, innovate, and elevate organizations. If their request is denied due to the focused desire to change, they will take their talents elsewhere, and the organizations they left will drown in exhaustion. Like the Mayor said, "the choice is life or death," Conflict Island or Growth Island.

create2elevate.com
BABY BOOMER/GEN X
survey:

Do you consider millennials the thought leaders in your company?

Yes	28%
No	72%

+6k Participants

A strategy2profit: Empower thought leaders

I have fallen in love with Belize, where I am honored to teach MBA courses for Galen University. As an instructor of amazing students in the entrepreneurship

111

track, I am privileged to teach innovation development, implementation strategies, qualitative and quantitative research development, thesis proposal, thesis research, and data analysis. Although I travel back and forth from Atlanta to the quaint town of San Ignacio, I've had extraordinary experiences throughout the nation.

On my first trip to Belize, I walked across an old wooden bridge that spans the width of the Macal River. The bridge connects the twin cities of San Ignacio and San Elaina. I was searching for a Belizean millennial who I wanted to interview for this research project. He had gone to England for a university education, but returned to Belize to open a tech-based exploration business in the mountains above San Elaina. Two hours into my hike, as I was on top of a mountain south of the town, I couldn't help but notice masses of intimidating black clouds on the horizon quickly approaching. Deciding to "beat" the clouds, I made a reckless decision to quickly walk back to the bridge in order to reach the safety of my hotel in San Ignacio.

Before I could reach the bridge, the mist had turned to monsoon-type rains that refused to yield to my desire for them to stop. Needless to say, I was not prepared for the rains, nor the flooding. Hoping to ride out the rains under a huge banyan tree adjacent to the river, I realized that the rains were not going to lighten up anytime soon. From my vantage point, I could see the low-lying wooden bridge over the river that would get me back to San Ignacio; however, the water level had already reached the underbelly of the bridge. Without hesitation, I made another reckless decision, I decided to go for it!

I did not factor that the wooden bridge would be extremely slippery when saturated with water. By the time I "skated" to the middle of the bridge, the water was coming over the top of the 1/4-mile-long structure. With just few hundred feet to reach the other side, the swift currents, coupled with the slippery wooden planks, swept my feet out from underneath me. Within a flash I had fallen and was thrown against the railing on the far-side of the bridge. The thin cable railing was the only thing that kept me from being carried down river.

Back to my feet and firmly holding onto the cable railing, I was thankful to reach the San Ignacio side, even in the relentless rains. In the far distance I could see a small structure with a front porch. When I reached the house, knowing that I was completely saturated in water, I thanked God for the stranger's porch where I had taken refuge.

After sitting on the porch for about 10 minutes, a sweet older lady emerged from inside. She brought me a cup of tea and a chocolate croissant. Patricia and I spoke for about an hour while the rains dissipated. She's a retired bakery owner that is greatly concerned about the future of Belize. Before I left, she asked me one question in her strong Spanish accent, "Kent, I am curious, why didn't you take the big bridge?" "What big bridge?" I asked. She said, "Look over there, that bridge!" Just a few hundred feet away from the old wooden bridge was a large suspension bridge far above the water level of the river. However, due to the reckless decisions in monsoon rains, I was blind to the bridge that would have ensured my safety.

Millennials have been called many things, but the firsthand voice in the surveys show that only 28% of BXers define millennials as "thought leaders" in their respective organizations. Acknowledging that demographic transitions have been happening since the advent of humanity, just being the largest population sect on the planet and possessing the largest annual purchasing power does NOT coronate millennials as "thought leaders." The undeniable variable that delineates millennials from all other demographics is NOT just the rate that technology is changing, but it is the modification that technology has had on human behavior. Methods, processes, engagement, relationship, and perspective have all been monumentally shifted due to technology.

While many BXers legitimately value their established channels of communication, face-to-face relationships, and meals with no cell phones; much of the millennial way of life is undergirded, driven, and defined by technology. However, the learning curve and time commitment required to maintain pace with rapidly changing technology is exhausting and cumbersome for the majority of BXers, but millennials, who know no other way of life; freely adapt, embrace, and grow with the changes.

While one demographic frets over the values that are being lost due to the influence of rapidly changing technology, another demographic is energized by the possibilities. Thus, **in order to secure the millennial customer base; you MUST be generating innovative ideas from employees who understand the behavioral patterns of the demographic.**

Although it may deeply grieve you to hear that millennials have been thrust to the front of your "thought leader" line; their innovation can become the cornerstones of your sustainable growth and profit for decades to come.

Further, do not make the same reckless decisions that I made. Due to the behavioral changes and structural modifications that millennials are embedding into organizational processes, the monsoon rains are just beginning. Be prepared and do not wait until it's too late. The river is swelling and will eventually cover the "tried and true" methods of growth and profit. Now is the time to build a bridge to millennials. Now is the time to empower millennial employees as *thought leaders*. Build the bridge high above the flood waters; the bridge is an intentional platform of voice to develop and articulate innovative ideas of relevance. Growth and profit go through millennial employees ... starting now!

Fearing millennial influence?

Suggesting that millennials are becoming the *thought leaders* in our organizational structures is NOT an insult to BXers. Actually, millennials recognize and respect that the innovation and growth that has been benefiting our corporate structures for many decades is the result of BXer ingenuity, intelligence, and discipline. There is no need to fear millennials; embrace their insights and perspectives of relevant growth.

---

create2elevate.com
BABY BOOMER/GEN X
survey:

If given a choice to earn $80k per year in a job with a consistent daily work schedule or $50k per year in a job that allows flexibility and creativity, which would you choose?

$80K	94%
$50K	6%

+6k Participants

create2elevate.com
MILLENNIAL
survey:

If given a choice to earn $80k per year in a job with a consistent daily work schedule or $50k per year in a job that allows flexibility and creativity, which would you choose?

$80K	27%
$50K	73%

+22k Participants

Critical Assessment:

BXers view this question through the lens of finance, while millennials view the question through the lens of flexibility. For a BXer to choose the $50k p/year position would be to abandon the ladder of success, and 94% state they are unwilling to prioritize flexibility over their "tried and true" ladder of success.

A strategy2profit: Reach for flexibility

Two years ago, I had a random conversation with a millennial CEO at a wedding reception. His tech company grew from 2 employees to 34 employees in 3 years. He attributes two key factors as the reason for his growth; the process used to hire employees and the flexibility offered once the employees are hired. His organizational theory was, "Happy employees = happy customers; happy customers = happy P/L statement."

The 32-year-old CEO stated, "Since I am a millennial, I understand what motivates my employees to excel. I offer them a schedule that some see as the blueprint for failure, but it has worked brilliantly for us. I require my employees to work in our building four hours per day, five days per week. But, between the hours of 8:00 AM and 6:00 PM, each employee is empowered to choose the four hours that work best for them and their lives. The other four hours of the day they can work anywhere or time they want. Every employee knows that we track their time and measure their productivity. If they fall short in our conditions of employment, they are terminated. But we have learned that the most productive and profitable time for our company is between 12:00-3:00 AM."

Inflexibility can forfeit profit. Four months after he told me this story, the company was purchased by a larger company with an older management team seeking to strengthen their market position. They quickly dissolved the flexible work schedules and forced the employees into a rigid work schedule of 8-5, Monday through Friday. Just prior to this book being published, I learned the company filed Chapter 11 bankruptcy and was aggressively seeking to hire employees to replace the ones that left. Again, "Happy employees = happy customers; happy customers = happy P/L statement." Jus say'in.

Based on the firsthand voice in the surveys, when offered a $80k per year job with a rigid schedule, or a $50k per year job with a flexible schedule; 7 of 10 millennials chose the $50k per year job. Selecting a job for $30k less per year is unfathomable to the generations prior to millennials. Once again, why is the millennial decision incomprehensible to non-millennials?

When non-millennials are given the option to choose a job that pays $50k or $80k per year, their lens of perspective is focused on security and accumulation. Whereas millennials read and interpret the question through a holistic lens; their answer is filtered through the priority of flexibility. Non-millennials see money first, millennials see flexibility first.

Seventy percent of millennials choose the lower paying position in order to have a flexible schedule. Although many BXers use the "flexibility" argument to construct a picture that suggests that millennials are "lazy and unwilling to pay the dues of success," the contrast in perspective is directly related to the ladder and the bridge.

From the "ladder of success" perspective, enduring and mastering routine is required to secure the next rung of growth on the ladder; I.e.: Rise at 5:30 AM, work, home, cable news, occasional date night with significant other, and a two-week vacation in July. Rigidity of routine is essential to success in the non-millennial model of growth.

Contrastively, the millennial bridge to growth is built on a holistic perspective that seeks the freedom to elevate the whole; I.e.: Being an active and present participant in the growth of self, family, community, nation, and planet. Yet, there is a critical point that

118

cannot be overlooked. By selecting the $50k job, millennials are NOT saying, "Give me money without working so that I can travel and save the world." Actually, millennials are saying that we want to work, earn a wage, and meet the needs of our families, but we also want flexibility to help others in need and fulfill a purpose that is greater than oneself.

A strategy2profit: Relinquish ownership of flexibility

Acknowledging that flexibility can be easy in theory and tough in reality, why not utilize the platform of voice to allow employees to create a structure of flexibility for employees and customers? Giving them ownership of the process will further reinforce your leadership legacy, elevate productivity, and fortify profit; which is a win-win-win for your organization.

The most consistent push back on flexible schedules that I hear at my conferences is from leaders in the healthcare, manufacturing, and service sectors. The most repetitive statement is, "Flexible schedules and methods will not work for our type of business!" Really? Have you given your employees the opportunity to figure out the matter? The data suggests that it's worth the effort if it elevates retention, productivity, secures growth, and fortifies profit.

Based on the +22k millennial voices in the survey, offering a flexible work schedule to your employees sends a definitive message that you care about the fulfillment of their purpose and trust them to take ownership of the processes that produce growth. In return, you receive a high level of productivity from satisfied employees seeking to elevate the whole, which includes your organization.

ENVY – or – RESPECT?

I confess that I hear an element of envy in the voice of non-millennials who are expressing their frustration regarding the millennial desire for a flexible schedule. However, where is the fault in sacrificing a higher wage in order to embrace a holistic perspective that seeks to actively elevate the whole?

If productivity and growth are the objectives…why not open the door for flexible work schedules?

create2elevate.com
MILLENNIAL
survey:

What is the optimum method of transportation to work?

Walk	38%
Drive	36%
Bike	26%

+6k Participants

create2elevate.com
BABY BOOMER/GEN X
survey:

What is the optimum method of transportation to work?

Drive	97%
Walk	2%
Bike	1%

+22k Participants

Strategy2profit: Position the customer

Utilizing real estate as an example, the four pieces of data that follow serve as a positioning guide beyond their face value. Noting the high priority that millennials place on flexibility; the companies, sectors, and organizations who intentionally position their customers in positions of flexibility are situated to profit with the millennial customer base. Noting that the surveys suggest that millennials are resistant to being locked into a long-term commitment, flexibility becomes a lens that millennials use to make significant financial decisions.

Take note in the shift in the "optimum mode of transportation" between BXers and millennials. The shift is not just about convenience and exercise, it's developed around flexibility. If millennials work close to their residence, they have more time to fulfill their personal purposes and holistic endeavors. Flexibility is strategic and intentional with millennials. This reality is emphatically substantiated in the following questions related to housing.

create2elevate.com
BABY BOOMER/GEN X

Where do you prefer to live?

Suburbs	64%
Rural Country	27%
City	9%

+6k Participants

create2elevate.com
MILLENNIAL
survey:

Where do you prefer to live?

City	44%
Rural Country	34%
Suburbs	22%

+22k Participants

Millennials are rejecting the suburbs and leading inner-city growth all over the world.[34] A mortgage banker in Miami recently told me that 45,000 condominiums and apartments are currently under construction in the city of Miami for 2019. No matter where I travel, I witness incredible growth happening in large and medium cities all over the world. Millennials are fueling that growth.

Millennials are determined to position themselves in environments that allow them to be flexible. However, the flexibility is not just developed around daily routines, flexibility is a lifestyle for millennials. To be tethered to a 30-year note that consumes the majority of their income is contradictive to the flexible lifestyle of millennials, which seems to be bad news for contractors, realtors, and mortgage bankers.

create2elevate.com
MILLENNIAL
survey:

If you had to choose between travel experiences and home ownership, which would you choose?

Travel experiences	62%
Home ownership	38 %

+22k Participants

---

[34] H. Lee, a Post-Doctoral fellow at Harvard suggests that this trend will continue into the unforeseeable future.
http://www.jchs.harvard.edu/blog/millennials-and-the-future-urban-landscape/ (Retrieved: 2/2019).

However, based on the data in the surveys, the bad news is solely developed around the traditional "tried and true" methods of growth.

Over the last 40 years, the prevailing method to purchase a home was predicated on the maximum limits of approval. A buyer would seek out an institution for a pre-approval, once the maximum amount of a mortgage was determined, the realtor and buyer would seek out homes according to the maximum qualified amount. In reality, homeowners were purchasing homes that maxed out their financial position. Thus, the size, scale, and location of the home was reflective of the identity of the people who lived inside.

Due to the priority of flexibility, the data shows that millennials reject the maxed out financial position for smaller homes and smaller mortgages.[35] Millennials aren't just more frugal than the generations before them, they are frugal with a purpose.

Therefore, the bad news is only bad if the "tried and true" methods are stubbornly maintained. If contractors, realtors, and mortgage bankers will strategically market and position millennials in financially flexible positions, they will thrive. The financial data that follows further substantiates this reality.

---

[35] The U.S. Federal Reserve report published in 2018 states; "Millennials have 42% less credit card debt and 13% smaller mortgage balances at the same stage of maturity." https://www.federalreserve.gov/econres/feds/files/2018080pap.pdf (Retrieved: 2/2019).

create2elevate.com
BABY BOOMER/GEN X

What are the top three priorities when seeking financial advice?

Savings retirement	34%
Personal finance	22%
Home ownership	22%
Start a business	17%
Student loan debt	3%
Rental property	2%

+6k Participants

create2elevate.com
MILLENNIAL
survey:

What are the top three priorities when seeking financial advice?

Student loan debt	41%
Personal finance	17%
Home ownership	16%
Rental property	16%
Savings retirement	8%
Start a business	2%

+22k Participants

Continuing to use real estate as an example of positioning millennials for profit. Beyond the staggering student loan debt, take note of the financial emphasis placed on rental property in the preceding question.[36] While BXers view rental property as the bottom priority in their financial priorities, millennials view rental property as an equal to home ownership. Millennials are purchasing small rental homes and duplex's for income streams, yet renting apartments and townhouses for their personal dwelling.

Since millennials want and value flexibility, they are content to rent while fortifying their financial position by purchasing a rental property. In the Fall of 2018, I met 34-year-old millennial named Bridget. Her father had just passed away and left her a sum of money. At the time that her father passed, she was living in an apartment in midtown Atlanta. Instead of purchasing herself a home or condo for a residence with her inheritance, she bought a rental property and remained in her apartment.

A few months later, I was the keynote speaker at EntreCon in Belize City. The millennial host told me the story about how she saved for 7 years to purchase a quadplex. After purchasing the property, she rented out all four units and remained in her apartment. Both Bridget and the Belizean gave me the same justification, we do not want to be tied down where our options are limited.

Based on the financial priorities revealed in the data; contractors, real estate agents, and mortgage bankers should be positioning millennials to purchase small rental properties. If BXers will strategically offer, promote, and

---

[36] A report published by the U.S. Treasury Department in 10.2018 states, "Student load debt in the U.S. is 1.52 trillion dollars." https://www.forbes.com/sites/zackfriedman/2018/06/13/student-loan-debt-statistics-2018/#b2fed177310f (Retrieved: 1/2019).

position themselves to accommodate the millennial customer base, they will be rewarded with profit. Further, the data in this project reveals that the same strategy2profit with can be applied in the manufacturing, financial services, and any other sector that is willing to strategically modify and embed their profit with flexibility.

create2elevate.com
BABY BOOMER/GEN X
survey:

Do you measure occupational achievement through company profit or fulfillment of purpose?

Profit	61%
Purpose	39%

+6k Participants

create2elevate.com
MILLENNIAL
survey:

Do you measure occupational achievement through company profit or fulfillment of purpose?

Profit	18%
Purpose	82%

+22k Participants

Critical Assessment:

The data suggests that "profit" is an integral component on each rung of the BXer ladder of success. If the aim of "profit" is achieved, the opportunity to climb to the next rung on the ladder is opened. Whereas, millennials see that the fulfillment of purpose as the optimum mode of achieving profit.

A strategy2profit: Engage passionate purpose

A strong theme of reality that I hear as I travel from city to city presenting the research is the unyielding pursuit of *purpose* by millennials. Although the fulfillment of *purpose* was not conjured up by a millennial drinking chai tea in an eclectic coffee shop, millennials have taken *purpose* to higher priority. Millennials are leaving high paying and prestigious jobs to pursue the fulfillment of individual *purpose*. This reality is illuminated in the question below from the millennial ONLY survey.

create2elevate.com
MILLENNIAL
survey:

If your employer would agree, would you give up a full-time position for a part-time position to pursue and fulfill your individual purpose?

YES	77%
NO	23%

+22k Participants

Millennials are not seeking an average *purpose*, they are reaching for a passionate *purpose*. They're passionate *purpose* carries such a deep conviction that nearly 8 of 10 are willing to relinquish the comfort and security of a full-time position in order to fully engage their passionate *purpose*. No matter the city or the organization, every time I present my research, I am approached and hear many inspiring stories about the pursuit of purpose from millennials, like the ones that follow. Even though I do not recall all their names, each of these people were eager to articulate their pursuit of passionate *purpose.*

A successful millennial wealth manager in Miami wanted to master the guitar in order to use his music for counseling and comfort for underprivileged kids. However, the time required to fully satisfy his passionate *purpose* conflicted with his demanding work schedule that made him the star in his region. He cautiously approached his boss with the idea, who instantly shot it down. Although he was aware that he was threatening his boss's income, he would not take "no" for an answer. He immediately proposed a trial period of three months, if production dropped or efficiency lacked, he would return to this full-time position. His boss reluctantly agreed to the proposal. One year later, his production was slightly down from his fulltime achievements, but still higher than on any other wealth manager in the region. He mastered the guitar and spent three hours per day traveling to mental facilities, juvenile retention centers, and halfway houses to play and counsel kids who had "fallen through the cracks." Today, his efforts are profiting the company who employs him, and the kids' lives he touches.

A millennial mortgage banker in Macon, Georgia was successfully guiding her city through a revitalization. After many decades of seeing historic and magnificent antebellum homes deteriorate and become an eyesore, she had a plan to change the trajectory of Macon. After putting together packages of grants and low interest loans to restore the homes to their former glory, she was able to create a market for the homes that would ultimately revitalize the downtown area. However, at the peak of her success, she informed her company that she wanted to change her status to part-time in order to pursue a "higher purpose." She wanted to become the best calligraphy writer in Macon. After seeing thousands of historical documents written in calligraphy, she realized that the stories, records, and identity of the city were being lost. She saw a need that would bring meaning to Macon. Today, as a part-time employee, her level of productivity for her employer has remained constant, and her calligraphy is the official font of Macon, Georgia. As she writes and preserves historical documents for the city that she loves, she is also fulfilling her passionate *purpose*.

A millennial lawyer at a top firm in Atlanta was deeply disturbed by "the derelict buildings and homeless people in his inner-city community." What no one in his firm knew, he was a closet artist who knew he had "a gift that was not being utilized to its fullest potential." Knowing he had a gift that could inspire and elevate his community, he scheduled an appointment with the senior partner to discuss the idea of working part-time. As with all the stories I hear, the immediate reaction was "no," but passion and reason have a convincing affect. Eighteen months later he had painted "murals with a message" on delipidated buildings, electrical boxes, and retaining walls. He told me, "I see the difference in attitudes, crime, and even property values. Also, other painters have joined my mission." When he was interviewed or sought out for advice, he made certain that people knew the name and mission of his firm that gave him the opportunity to engage his passionate *purpose*. As a result, he said, "The firm's top clients still request me to represent them. They respect my mission and what I stand for, which resonates with them. My firm has greatly benefited with growth, profit, and publicity by allowing me to fulfill my purpose."

131

Every city, state, and country where I present the research, I hear more of these stories, but it is not by accident or coincidence that each of the companies who employee these part-time millennials are still benefiting greatly from their service. This research project strongly suggests that if organizations will prioritize the passionate *purpose* of their millennial employees over profit, the organization ultimately grows and profits greater from committed employees who appreciate the opportunity to fulfill their *purpose*.

Every leader that I have spoken to about this phenomenon has communicated the same message to me, their millennial employees who transitioned to part-time are nearly as productive as they were as full-time employees. However, the attention, publicity, and goodwill returned to the organization has been far greater than anyone expected. Furthermore, by allowing the employees to fulfill their passionate *purpose*, the organizations retain their top talent, which secures growth and profitability. Give your millennials a chance to pursue their passionate *purpose*, then watch your growth and profit expand.[37]

---

[37] See section titled, *Holistic Capital*

SNAPSHOT of understanding:

Clarity

The millennial desire to have a flexible work schedule is NOT about traveling to exotic destinations to participate in sunrise yoga; it is about being present and active in the local community.

Should I, or Should I not?

A platform of voice is NOT ...
> a form of entitlement or placating to millennials.

A platform of voice IS ....
> an astute structure of sustainable growth.

A strategy2profit: Create experiential environments

Irrespective of the culture or nation, purchasing a home communicates a loud message of stability, discipline, and growth; which is why BXers are astonished that 62% of millennials choose travel experiences over home ownership. Further enflaming the conflict of perspective, 80% of BXers prioritize the "stability" of home ownership over travel experiences, explicitly communicating a priority of fiscal responsibility. Although the face value of the question indicates that millennials are content with financial irresponsibility, yet the firsthand voice in the survey illuminates a different reality.

A frequent and frustrated statement that I hear following my conferences, "Millennials choose travel experiences over home ownership because they will inherit my home! Why would they buy a home if they are going to inherit mine?" Actually, there is an element of truth to that reality, but it is a minimal part of the equation. The heart of the millennial response is not about home ownership; it is about the definition of "stability."

Millennials look beyond the obsession of individual stability to focus on a holistic stability; one that seeks to embed health and depth into the individual, family, community, culture, and planet as a whole unit. From the millennial perspective, stabilizing one while ignoring the others is to destabilize the whole.

For 62% of the millennial voices in the survey, home ownership is viewed as enslavement to one small spot of life that serves as an impediment to holistic growth and stability. Further, the majority of millennials place a higher priority on the depth gained from

135

experiential opportunities over the interest and debt required to stabilize one small spot of existence. In other words, home ownership is viewed as a threat to holistic stability and an infringement to experiential opportunities.

This perspective is further understood by the next question in the survey.

create2elevate.com
MILLENNIAL
survey:

Do you prefer to spend your money on an experience or a product of comfort?

Experience	69%
Product of comfort	31%

+22k participants

The sub-question imbedded in this question states,
FINANCIAL PRIORITY: If you had $2,000 and needed a couch, would you use the $2,000 to purchase a new couch, or spend $200 on a used couch and use the balance for an experiential adventure?

To all non-millennial leaders seeking growth with millennial employees and customers, etch this point deep in your decision-making processes; millennials define the depth gained from experiential opportunities as one of the highest forms of stability. Moving forward, wise leaders will incorporate experiential opportunities into the workplace, housing communities, restaurants, schools, and all other areas seeking growth with millennials.

SNAPSHOT for Profit:

Position2profit

Use an intentional platform of voice to strategically position your millennial employees to:

- establish relevancy with the millennial customer base,
- transition to thought leaders,
- develop models of flexibility, and
- fulfill their passionate purpose.

In return, you'll position your customer base to secure growth and fortify profit.

CHAPTER #3 REVIEW: A strategy2profit

Per the data, there are 4 essential components for a strategy2profit with millennials:

1. Product lines and marketing must be relevant to millennials. The only way to establish relevancy is through an intentional platform of voice.

2. Empower millennials to become the thought leaders. Empowering comes through an environment that allows millennials to develop and generate innovative ideas of value.

3. Position millennial employees and customers with flexibility. BXers should allow millennials to develop and generate models of flexibility through a platform of voice.

4. Position millennial employees and customers to engage their passionate purpose.

Chapter 4

need2do-NOW

urgent action required

No time like…NOW!

After being seated in a respected restaurant in Athens, Georgia, our millennial waiter came to the table requesting our drink order. Knowing that we were celebrating a grueling accomplishment that had physically and mentally exhausted us, we selected a bottle of fine Pinot Noir. A few minutes later, the waiter hastily placed the uncorked and half full bottle of wine on our table as he passed to take an order from another customer. Confused by the waiter's actions, we chose to "go with the flow" and enjoy our moment of celebration. A few minutes later, the waiter drops by the table and asks, "How's your bottle of wine?" Trying not to be shocked by his naivety, with a smile and respectful tone I responded, "Considering that it was open, half full, and we have no glasses to pour it in, we haven't had a chance to taste it." Instantly the young man teared up and walked away. A few minutes later, the genX manager comes over to apologize and informs us that we have a new waiter.

Having intentionally steered clear of personal perspectives on millennials throughout this book, in the spirit of transparency I will inject a personal position that I held prior to developing the project. As a BXer, I observed what I perceived to be entitled, lazy, and selfish millennials, but I also witnessed creative, energetic, and innovative pursuits from millennials. I was disgusted and enamored all at the same time.

As with many researchers who develop comprehensive projects, I did not envision outcomes that existed outside my personal perspectives. Based on the outcomes in this project, I can confidently declare that personal perspectives were errant, and millennials will be one of the greatest generations in organizational history.[38]

Before millennials start celebrating by moving the sofa to the back yard with growlers and a fire pit, I can also report that millennials have two significant deficits in critical areas of organizational fluidity; customer service and task failure. Beyond a platform of voice that elevates retention, heightens talent acquisition, and generates innovative ideas of value, both of those areas require intense and immediate attention from organizational leaders...NOW!

---

[38] See the section in this chapter titled, "Will millennials be the greatest generation in organizational history?

create2elevate.com
BABY BOOMER/GEN X
survey:

What is the is most effective method to communicate financial or educational advice?

Face to face	38%
Email	26%
Telephone	26%
Text	4%
You Tube	4%
Podcast	1%
Social Media	1%

+6k Participants

create2elevate.com
MILLENNIAL
survey:

What is the is most effective method to communicate financial or educational advice?

Podcast	23%
Social Media	23%
Email	14%
Text	12%
You Tube	12%
Face to face	9%
Telephone	7%

+22k Participants

create2elevate.com
BABY BOOMER/GEN X
survey:

What is the optimum mode of customer service?

Face to face	39%
Telephone	31%
Email	26%
Podcast	1%
Social Media	1%
Text	1%
You Tube	1%

+6k Participants

create2elevate.com
MILLENNIAL
survey:

What is the optimum mode of customer service?

Social Media	23%
Podcast	23%
Email	14%
Text	12%
You Tube	12%
Face to face	9%
Telephone	7%

+22k Participants

Critical Assessment:
BXers and millennials define and prioritize effective channels of communication from vastly different perspectives. As a result, communication is a core component in the conflict between BXers and millennials.

Growth can be a placebo that blinds us to pockets of dysfunction. That is precisely what happened to one of my top clients. Their revenue had increased for 8 consecutive years. Each of those years their employee and customer base had gradually increased. As a result, the leadership celebrated their fluid and productive structure with bonuses, conferences, and other fringe benefits. Yet, while they were basking in their achievement, there was an undetected cancer that was slowly eating away at their organizational foundation. When discovered, the diagnosis was a subtle and aggressive form of cancer called customer service.

A need2do-NOW: Save customer service

Based on the outcomes of the surveys, and volumes of concerned organizational leaders, I have strongly encouraged companies to take immediate action regarding millennials and customer service. Recognizing that customer service positions are typically the first face or voice of the organization, customer service dysfunction impedes growth, creates conflict, and strengthens the competition. Yet, millennials seem to be taking customer service to all time low.

144

By default, most customer service positions are defined as entry level positions. Entry level positions are typically given to the younger demographics who are just beginning their career. Today, customer service positions are overwhelmingly filled by millennials, specifically younger millennials.

Although I would NEVER define millennials as a cancer, there are two realties revealed in the survey that significantly threaten growth regarding customer service and millennials. First, the age of adulthood; millennials define the age of adulthood as 28 years old.[39] Based on that reality, do you want the first face and voice of your organization to be one that sees themselves as a kid? Further, do you want kids solving complicated and continuous issues for your longstanding and valued clients? Last, do you want kids as a determining factor in your sustainable growth?

Second, as we discussed in the strategy2profit chapter, only 7% of millennials define the telephone as the optimum mode of communication. While 70% of BXers state that face-to-face or a telephone is the optimum mode of communication.

Customer service is dependent on communication; however, BXers and millennials define effective commination vastly different, which creates outcomes of conflict that can be detrimental to growth and profit.

- 70% of BXers state that face-to-face or a telephone call is the optimum method of customer service (create2elevate NON-millennial survey)

---

[39] From a marketing perspective, is it fiscally responsible to market adult products and services to millennials who do not see themselves as an adult?

- 75% of baby boomers and gen X think calling is the most effective way to get a response (NewVoice)
- 66% of millennials state that social media and Podcast are the optimum method of customer service (create2elevate millennial ONLY survey)
- 39% of millennials first go to a company's FAQ page when they have a question (Salesforce)

It seems that many view customer service departments life referees, no one takes notice of them, unless they make a mistake. However, customer service is a key component to *growth* and *profit*, yet, the traditional model of customer service is greatly *threatened* by the millennial perspective of effective channels of communication.

Growth through customer service:
- 77% expect to grow due to excellent customer service. (Deloitte)
- 40% of customers begin purchasing from a competitor because of their reputation for great customer service.
- 24% of customers continue to seek out companies for 2+ years following a positive customer service experience. (Zendesk)

Profit through customer service:
- 58% are willing to spend more money with companies that provide excellent customer service. (American Express)
- 51% of customers use a company more frequently after a positive customer service experience. (NewVoice)

- 62% of companies view customer service as a key competitive differentiator. (Deloitte)

Threatened by poor customer service:
- 82% of consumers have stopped doing business with a company due to bas customer service. (Zendesk)
- 66% of customers switch companies due to poor customer service. (Accenture)
- 45% of customers switch to a competitor following a poor customer service experience. (NewVoice)
- 58% will never use a company again due to a bad customer service experience.
- 59% of 25-34-year-old millennials get revenge by posting a bad review online. (NewVoice)

As you see from the data in create2elevate surveys and other outside sources, customer service defines your residency; is it Conflict Island or Growth Island? A permanent residency on Conflict Island is the result of ignoring the conflict or defaulting to the "tried and true" methods to solve the issue. A permanent residency on Growth Island comes from taking action based on the data in the surveys. Stop trying to solve the problem through BXer lenses, create a platform of voice that will generate innovative ideas of value that fortify customer service. Utilize the creative, innovative, and insightful voices of your millennials to elevate the customer service experience. Your growth and profit are dependent upon your response to the conflict in customer service.

A need2do-NOW: Tackle task failure

Organized extracurricular activities for kids in the Caribbean are sparse. In 2008, I was honored to start a kid's football league on St John, U.S. Virgin Islands. After three seasons, the league was the island wide social event every Friday night. Droves of people filled the stands and lined the fences along the field in downtown Cruz Bay.

As with all competitive leagues, we played a full season, followed by the playoffs to crown the divisional champion. In our fourth season, our 11&12-year-old championship was a hard-fought game that went into double overtime. With the stands filled with proud parents and cheering fans, the kids gave everything they had to win the game. The game ended in the most dramatic fashion, a team stopped the other team six inches from the goal line. One team laid on the ground crying in defeat, while the other was ecstatically celebrating their season long achievement.

Within seconds of the game finishing, I had an angry parent in my face demanding that all the kids get a championship trophy. When I said, "I'm sorry, but one team won and the other lost, that's the way life works." The parent went into an irate tantrum shouting and cursing. She screamed at me, "Look over there at those kids! They're balling their eyes out! They all deserve a championship trophy! You're causing irreputable damage to those kids!" Really? I thought I was teaching them a life lesson.

As I walked away, I wondered if she'd be acting the same way if her kid's team would have won? I wondered if she'd be concerned about the trophies for the other kids if the outcome was reversed? Based on her behavior, I doubted it. All she could see was that her

148

kid's team fell six inches short and lost the game. Her son was laying on the field crying, and she was coming to his emotional rescue. By demanding a championship trophy, she was communicating to her kid that losing had the same reward as winning.

Based on that experience, I wonder how that young man, who is now 20 years old, is handling task failure in the work place? Is he expecting a pat on the back when he fails, or does he go off somewhere to cry until his boss pacifies him with a reward?

C-Suite execs and management teams are communicating a consistent message to me, the smallest of task failures are prompting millennials to quit their jobs. Instead of enduring the short-lived correction due to a task failure, many millennials are quitting and moving on to the next job.

Knowing that my data driven mission is to ask the question "Why," the answer is always the same; "Millennials are the 'trophy' generation!" Yet, my reply always goes back to that football field in Cruz Bay, "Who's fault is it that they expect a trophy for losing? Is it theirs? No, it's the generations before them that could not bear to see their child fail. Although millennials have been widely referred to as the "entitled and trophy" generation, I can confidently state that BXers are the enabler generation.

Task failure plays a significant role in millennial retention rates. If you are sincerely reaching for growth and profitability with millennial employees and customers, your organizational structure must proactively coach millennials through the failure process. Further, based on the outcomes from the create2elevate platform of voice, the response to task failure is dramatically improved throughout the organization. The collaborative and competitive component embedded in the

149

create2elevate structure means that a few will win, while the majority will fall short. However, the collaborative environment means that everyone is accountable for their responses and actions. For a millennial who was not allowed to fail, accountable and collaborative failure is the most effective method to teach fortitude.

A need2do-NOW: Stop collaborative dysfunction

A structural change sweeping across the corporate landscape is the emphasis placed on collaborative environments. Last year I was invited to discuss my research to a company executive at the Chick-fil-a headquarters just outside of Atlanta. As I toured the six-story facility nestled in a beautiful rolling forest, I was overwhelmed by the priority and commitment to collaboration.

To reinforce the commitment and *serve* the employees as authentic leaders, the C-Suite offices were relocated from traditional walled offices on the sixth floor to unwalled environments on the first floor. Following the relocation, all the interior walls on five of the six floors were removed or replaced with glass encasements. Throughout the entire building, there are collaborative spaces, cafes, coffee shops, and technology that promotes collective achievement. If you've ever had the privilege of eating at one of the Chick-fil-a franchises, you've probably witnessed that the model established at the leadership level is emulated throughout the entire organization.

As efficient and productive environments of collaboration continue to be developed, we must also be aware that there are collaborative relationships that destabilize and threaten the growth of organizations. One of those relationships has been illuminated in this chapter.

Task failure among millennials is directly related to the communication deficit. Based on the +22k voices in the millennial ONLY survey, only 16% of the respondents define face-to-face or a telephone call as the optimum mode of communication and customer service conflict resolution. Therefore, when millennials are positioned in customer service positions that are traditionally defined by the telephone and/or face-to-face conflict resolution, millennials are overwhelmingly resistant, due to the deficiency in their respective skillsets. In other words, based on the data, leaders who position millennials in customer service positions that are developed around the telephone and/or face-to-face relationships, are setting their millennial employees up for task failure.

The collaborative relationship between task failure and customer service with millennials is an issue that must be intentionally and aggressively addressed in order to secure growth and fortify opportunity with millennial employees and customers. However, BXer leaders continue to make the same errant mistake regarding this matter. STOP TRYING TO SOLVE THE PROBLEM THROUGH YOUR LENS OF PERSPECTIVE! Stop the training processes! Stop hiring consultants to "fix the problem." Stop trying to solve the issue through the "tried and true" methods. The only way you're going to solve these issues is through your millennial employees. Relinquish your role as the problem solver, empower your millennial employees to solve the problem by providing them with an intentional platform of voice. The collaborative and competitive environment will solve the problem.

A need2do-NOW: Leader or enabler?

During the Q&A period of my research presentation in Sunrise, Florida, a millennial named Travis stood up to address the customer service/communication issue. Although I'm certain that the throngs of BXers in attendance assumed he was about to defend the deficits, he communicated a brilliant analogy.

He told a story about playing baseball as a young kid. The first year I played as a 5-year-old, most of our games ended in a 0-0 tie. Since very few kids could hit the ball when pitched from as pitcher, there were rarely runs scored. The next year the parent association decided that the games would be more fun if the ball was not pitched, but hit off a T. The T helped a little, but very few runs were being scored. Halfway through the season, the same parent association modified the rules and decided that we did not have to hit the ball off the T. The new rules stated that we could hit anywhere on the T, if the ball was fair, we could run to first base. Instead of teaching us to hit the ball from the pitcher, which was the way it would be as we grew older, our parents could not stand the thought of us falling. What lesson did we learn? If we can't hit the ball, our parents will fix it for us. Does that equate to real life?"

BXers must determine if they are going to enable, judge, or lead millennial employees. *Enable* has emphatically produced an environment of task failure and communication deficits. *Judgment* has pushed away top millennial talent. *Leaders* solve problems through effective methods that produce growth outcomes. As you know well by now, the data strongly suggest that giving millennial employees a voice to solve critical issues within the organizational structures is the solution. A platform of voice is the solution.

One of my first clients was being ravaged by the dysfunctional collaboration of customer service and communication deficits with millennial employees. Unsuccessfully, they spent over a hundred thousand dollars in consultant fees and training programs to solve the issue. Yet, when they implemented the outcomes in this research and allowed the employees to solve the issue through the create2elevate platform of voice, the result was immediate.

As group after group presented their ideas at the event, one idea stood out above all others. The idea was to place only gen Xers as the first voice and face of the company. Upon engagement with a customer, their sole mission was to determine if they were speaking to a boomer, gen Xer, or a millennial. Based on their conclusions, they would send millennial customers only to millennial customer service representatives, BXer customers only to BXer customer service reps. The millennials developed effective methods to communicate with other millennials, while BXers used their tried and true methods on BXers. One year later, the company has solved many of their customer services issues and most of their communication issues; yet most importantly, they secured their growth and fortified profit with satisfied customers and fulfilled employees.

THE SOLUTION!

What does an intentional platform of voice that seeks to generate innovative ideas of value accomplish?

1. Employee generated ideas that become cornerstones of sustainable growth
2. Secured profit
3. Elevated employee retention
4. Top talent attraction and acquisition
5. Relevance with customer base
6. Employee engagement by seizing ownership of processes
7. Employees fulfilling their purpose
8. Self-growth
9. Equality and organizational fluidity for all
10. A solid legacy of leadership
11. Active presence in the local community
12. Elevated morale and productivity

Secure growth and fortify profit with millennial employees and customers.

Do not blow this opportunity!

Apply for residency on Growth Island

There is only one condition to becoming a resident on Growth Island; build a bridge, which is an intentional platform of voice for your employees to generate innovative ideas of value. As a leader, you can either surrender on Conflict Island, or be celebrated on Growth Island.

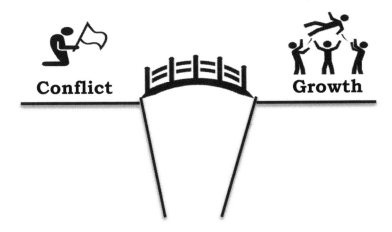

Appendix A

Case study: Conflict Island or Growth Island?

I lived in the Caribbean for over 20 years. My first island home was Jamaica, where I served as the Managing Director of the Institute of the Caribbean. After accepting the position, I sold my software training business, closed up my house in Georgia, and relocated to the rural mountains above Ocho Rios.

The school is located on the property of the 300-year-old Lyford Park Great House, built by Sir Alfred DeCosta. British royalty, Jamaican Prime Ministers, Afro-Carib athletes, and renowned scholars have used the home for many of the most historic galas in the Caribbean. Characterizing the 10-bedroom house as an architectural marvel is to understate its magnificence.

Three hundred years of foot traffic are worn into 8,000 square-feet of dark mahogany planks on the floor. The giant tapered mahogany columns that border the stately living room support the thirty-foot high ornamental ceilings. The steeped pitched metal roof is appropriately painted royal green to symbolize the fullness of life that emanates throughout the island, but it's the geographical position sets the house apart from all others.

Proudly positioned on the peak of a majestic countryside mountaintop, each morning the valleys below fill with fog, giving the impression that the house is floating on a cloud. As the morning fog slowly dissipates, the 360° view of the valleys below reveal a vibrant tropical foliage that perfectly illustrates the splendor of the island. After the sun sets behind the lush mountains, a crisp evening breeze threads its way throughout every room in the house, defusing the worries of the day and easing the anxieties of tomorrow.

Visitors from all around the world have fittingly used "Majestic" as the adjective to describe the setting, which is why I was shocked when a local businessman warned me of imminent conflict. He said to me, *"This nation is at a crossroads—the days ahead will be remembered by either growth or conflict. Knowing what I know about our leaders, prepare the school for what is about to come. No matter how strong you perceive our nation to be, I see conflict beginning to saturate all the elements of our culture! Mark my word, every leader on this island will be measured by how they respond to this conflict."*

Based on the strength of the culture, beauty of the island, and 3 million tourists who spend their money in Jamaica every year; my skeptical response was, "What conflict?"

The conflict

In spite of its magnificent beauty, rich culture, and strong tourism sector, the Jamaican population outside of Jamaica is greater than the population on the island. For 50 consecutive years no region in the world has had a higher migration rate away from the region than the Caribbean. Although it's a confounding reality, why would high volumes of people leave "paradise?" For the same reasons that high volumes of millennials are leaving well-paying jobs every 18 months.

Each year thousands of Jamaicans assess reality and determine that their creative, passionate, and innovative ideas will never be respected or developed on Conflict Island. As a result, they migrate until they find a structure that respects and facilitates their creative, passionate, and innovative ideas of value.

158

Conflict Island vs. Growth Island
Case study analysis: **WHAT?**

WHAT conflict in "paradise?" I.e.: WHAT conflict in your company?

While Jamaican leaders scoff at the notion of conflict in "paradise," they resolutely prioritize their product of tourism over environments that would generate unique and profitable innovation from their residents. Although each visitor to the island represents another dollar of revenue, each resident that leaves represents innovative ideas that are developed and implemented elsewhere. In other words, the decision not to prioritize the innovative voice of their millennial residents is strengthening their competition. Thus, the conflict is self-inflicted and directly correlated to leaders that stubbornly hold onto an errant perspective, "If we keep doing the same things we've always done, things will work themselves out." However, the conflict has not worked itself out and is *the* reason why the island is drowning in financial crisis and hemorrhaging its innovative, creative, and smart millennial work force.[40] Ironically, Jamaican leaders blame the nation's economic struggles on the "lazy, selfish, and entitled" youth; yet the "youth" passionately believe their relevant and innovative ideas can be the cornerstones of growth for decades to come. Tragically, the lost revenue from innovative residents that migrate from Jamaica has long surpassed the revenue of tourism.

---

[40] Findings in *Wessinger, K. (2016). The relationship between creative practice and socioeconomic crisis in the Caribbean: A path to sustainable growth. Routledge: London, UK.*

159

After presenting my research to the executive team of a globally recognized manufacturing company, the CFO made a crass comment, "We must be the anomaly to your research, our millennials love working here." Without hesitation, the CEO turned to the HR Director and asked, "What is our retention rate with millennial employees?" Her response, "Since I have never been asked that question, we've never seen the need to track the retention rates of millennials." Although I wanted to drop the mic and make a dramatic exit, we all sat there stunned by the revelation.

Two months later, the CEO called and asked me to return to discuss solutions to their millennial retention rates. He told me, "We are consistently ranked as one of the top employers in the world and our product lines remain healthy, but I will not be guilty of sticking my head in the sand and pretending that we do not have a conflict with millennial employees. Since our last meeting, I learned that our millennial employees worldwide remain employed by us an average of 23 months. I see that as a serious concern and threat to our growth."

Utilizing the data in the surveys to further unpack the conflict, 73% of the 22k+ millennial voices in this project reveal there *is* a conflict related to employee retention, yet 61% of the 6k+ BXers state there is *no* conflict.[41] Millennials migrate from job to job at an average of every 18 months; whereas Gen X is 9.2 years,

---

[41] Data from the c2e Millennial ONLY Survey and NON-millennial Survey. Question #6 in the NON-millennial Survey states, "Is millennial retention negatively affecting your company or organization?"

and baby boomers 19.1 years.[42] Although the data illuminates an escalating conflict that threatens stability, many organizational leaders are asking, "What conflict?" Innovative, creative, and smart millennial employees are migrating from company to company in record numbers, the chapters that follow analyze *why* they are migrating.

Conflict Island vs. Growth Island
Case study analysis: **WHERE?**

Where do Jamaicans go when they leave their island? I.e.: Where are your millennials going when they leave your organization?

The names of the countries that Jamaicans migrate too are not important. The rank and file Jamaican perspective is defined by one objective; abandon Conflict Island for Growth Island! It should be noted that Jamaicans do not want to leave Jamaica. They passionately desire to be active participants in sustainable growth, but the failure from political leaders to wisely respond to the conflict has pushed them to Growth Island, which further heightens the conflict on Conflict Island.

The firsthand voice in the surveys reveal that your millennial employees do not want to leave your organization. However, when they leave, they utilize their creative, innovative, passionate, progressive talents to secure growth and profitability to competitors who value their innovative insights.[43]

---

[42] Data from the c2e Millennial ONLY Survey and NON-millennial Survey.
[43] There is a case study in Chapter 6 that specifically addresses millennial migration and the leverage provided to competitors.

The failure of Jamaican leaders to respond with environments of development and growth transformed the conflict into a full-blown crisis. Yet, the U.S., Canada, and England are financial benefactors of Jamaican innovation and leadership from those who have migrated.

Who is benefiting when your creative and innovative millennial employees who migrate to other organizations? Not you!

No matter the nation or the sector, millennials repetitively tell me the same story, *"After being on the job for a year, I identified a solvable impediment to growth. Because my methods and approach were different than the way things had always been done, I was not given the time, tools, or environment to develop the idea. When I saw no hope of growth, I took my methods and ideas to a competitor who financially benefited from my desire to participate in growth."*

Noting that, "entitled, lazy, and selfish" are not attributes of achievement, more than 80% of the BXer voices in this project definitely suggest that millennials are not high achievers. Yet, millennials are the growth leaders in the 3 fastest growing sectors in the global economy; technology, energy, and green construction.[44] While millennials are already reconstituting the organizational structures in the financial services sector, education, and tech, the outcomes in this project strongly suggests that millennials will reconstitute structures and processes in all sectors in the next two decades.

Conflict Island or Growth Island?
Case study summation:

---

[44] (World Bank, 2017)

Millennials are changing jobs on average of every 18 months.[45] At the 12-month mark millennial employees have assessed the structure and made a decision to remain or leave.[46] Recognizing that millennial retention rates are the worse of any demographic ever recorded, you're beginning to see that the migration of your millennial employees is reaching crisis mode and negatively affecting your fluidity, growth, and profit.[47] Each of my corporate clients are communicating the same frustrated scenario; "We are hemorrhaging millennial employees, our training budgets are exploding, filling open positions with millennial talent is a quandary, growth is being destabilized, and profit is being threatened."

Thus, you are faced with two monumental decisions; the first is to cling to your opinion of "entitled, lazy, and selfish" and remain on Conflict Island or build a bridge to Growth Island. BXer leadership moving forward will be measured by the answer to one question; "Can you generate cornerstones of sustainable growth through the innovative, creative, and progressive talents of your millennial workforce?"

"You can create a future with millennials,
OR…millennials will create a future for you!"

APPENDIX B
Risk management…with millennials

---

[45] c2e Millennial ONLY Survey
[46] Ibid.
[47] Gallup suggests that millennial turnover costs the U.S. economy $30.5 billion annually (5/2016).

Do millennials represent high risks?

The Internet is saturated with opinions that boldly suggest that millennials are the most "risk adverse" generation ever recorded; yet the firsthand voice in the surveys emphatically indicate otherwise. If risk is viewed through the traditional litigious lens, millennials are definitely "risk adverse" in contrast to the two generations that precede them. However, when risk is viewed through the lens of retention, continuity, and growth; millennials possess the highest risk factor(s) ever recorded.

Noting that millennials will reconstitute structures and processes considered absolute; now is the time to identify, measure, assess and prioritize millennial variables of "risk management" that secure accurate economic outcomes.

Are millennials astute risk managers?

The 3 variables that constitute an accurate evaluation of risk are identification, measurement, and assessment. Each of 3 variables are embedded in the core of millennial retention, which defines millennials as astute and methodical risk managers.

Millennials strategically "identify" a company that seemingly meshes with their passion and skill set. After one-year of employment, they have sufficiently "measured the probability" of developing and implementing their innovative ideas of value. If they "assess" that the probability is low, they will take "control" of their environment by moving to the next company.

APPENDIX C
Could millennials be the greatest generation in organizational history?

Consider this:
1. Holistic Capital

Due to the methods required to climb the ladder of success, capital has been compartmentalized. Some are determined to build financial capital, while others are driven to build social, people, instructional, and natural capital. Yet, millennials feel so strongly about building holistic capital that they will take less money, make great sacrifices, and migrate from job to job until they find a place to elevate the whole.

The overwhelming majority of millennials do not seek to marginalize nor discriminate. Their resolute desire for equality, service, and environment is fortifying a foundation of healthy and sustainable growth. As a result, holistic capital is becoming the most treasured form of development and wealth on the planet.

2. Mission Driven

Recognize that millennials have an uncompromising resolve to collaboratively elevate the whole. Millennials are mission driven, not position driven, which is why millennials reject ladders and embrace bridges. From a millennial perspective, position is not success, bridges of purpose that elevate the whole define success. "Position" sacrifices the greater good for self-interests, while "mission" sacrifices self-interests for the greater good.

3. Present

Millennials possess a great resolve to fulfill their mission, which is to holistically elevate the whole. Millennials are willing to sacrifice position and pay to be present and active in their mission.

Additional factors: Education with a holistic purpose, empty buckets, and enthusiasm to embrace rapidly changing behavioral patterns.

You can create a future with millennials, OR millennials will create a future for you!

-OR-

One outcome will fortify your legacy as a *champion* of leadership and growth, while the other will perpetuate conflict and force you to *surrender*.

THE END....

Made in the USA
Columbia, SC
27 June 2019